CONTENTS

CW00450172

Three Stripes, I'm Out

FOREWORD

I was labelled a rebel at home and at school by my teachers and was once told by my Year Head, that I would not last five minutes in the military.

I was 16 years old and had a point to prove! I decided to turn my life around, so I joined the Royal Air Force. Three years later I found myself as part of the Task Force heading 8000 miles to liberate the Falkland Islands in the South Atlantic.

This is my recollection and memories from all those years ago; yet I have trouble remembering events from more recent times. I hope that some of the humour and accounts will bring back memories to any ex-servicemen or women reading this.

Over forty years ago, I stepped onto a train to take me to RAF Swinderby in Lincolnshire. This was a journey that was to change the rest of my life.

I met my wife Imelda when I was 14, she was my best friends' girlfriend; I was seeing his sister. Imelda and I started seeing each other straight away, though she was due to go on holiday to Ireland for the summer with her parents. Whilst she was away, I started looking into the idea of joining the Royal Air Force (RAF). Imelda knew that I had aspired to join up and she gave me her full support during my career and then with my transition into civvy street.

My son Patrick liked my stories so much, he made me write this book. So, I am telling my story to him, my daughter Tamara, and my grandchildren. Some of my family and friends are also mentioned here.

Fortunately, I have made many friends over the years and through social media, I am still able to be in contact with most of them. My friends' list includes friends from my infant school through secondary education and my time in the Royal Air Force (RAF).

Some of the language is strong, but that's how it was. If you don't feel offended, read on, if you do, why not give it a go, you might get to understand what life can be like in the military.

INTRODUCTION

The Falklands War, the Cold War, and N.A.T.O Operations
– this is my story:

I was born to Anglo Indian parents who emigrated to England in the early 1960s, my dad was the 2nd youngest in a family of eight boys and six older sisters. My grandfather, who was a descendant of the Campbell clan from the Scottish Highlands was gold miner chargehand in the Mika Mines in Kolar Gold Fields, Bangalore or KGF India, as it is commonly known.

My nan on my dad's side, was murdered after being poisoned by a neighbour following a dispute. My grandad was killed in a mining accident one evening when they were blasting rocks. I am not sure what nan's dispute was about, but I remember my dad telling me, that grandad was doing a controlled explosion using dynamite to blast some rocks. A boulder broke loose and was about to fall; he saw that there was a young Tamil worker underneath, so my grandad ran in and pushed him out of the way and saved his life; unfortunately, my grandad was killed in the process.

This affected my dad in a big way, but it helped him to make his decision and not follow in his fathers' footsteps, but instead, he was to join the Indian Army as a despatch rider. My dad used to tell some of the tales of his few years in the army, and he also confessed that he was once "court martialed", but he never said why.

My dad had already met my mum through a family friend but there was a seven-year age gap between them; mum was 17 and still in school and dad was 24.

They eventually married on Boxing Day in 1960 just before my mum turned 19. They came to England by ship along with my mum's sister and moved into rented accommodation in Wembley. I was then born in 1962.

Three Stripes, I'm Out

We were living in a house on London Road just a stone throws away from Wembley Stadium. Then in late 1966 (just after the world cup final), I can honestly say I was in Wembley at that time; dad got a job in a factory in Croydon, South London, but this meant relocating. My late father, Patrick's, influence on my life made my journey truly wonderful. He would often come home from work and talk about his day; I would put the kettle on, and he would say to me "How was your day son?" and I would tell all that had happened to me. We were very close. I suppose being an only child, I looked up to him as my older brother.

CHAPTER 1

Early Days and Career Choice.

Three Stripes, I'm Out

During my upbringing, one of the legacies passed on to me was music. My parents and all my aunts and uncles were seriously into fifties rock 'n' roll in particular, Elvis Presley. My dad used to listen to rock n roll music all the time and I came to enjoy it, so one day with a circle of friends including my future wife, we started going to pubs and clubs dressed in the full fifties attire complete with the mandatory "ducks arse" haircut. With this "uniform" despite us being only 14 or 15 years old, most of us passed as being over 18, though I do not recollect ever being ID checked.

Back in 1976, I was in a gang, we were all aged between 11 and 14 years old; when I say gang, I mean a circle of friends. We never got in trouble, we never caused trouble, but admittedly, we were a little noisy at times and one of us may have even put a football or 2 accidentally through someone's window. One day we were accused of terrorising some of the locals, the Croydon Advertiser ran a story with the headline "They're Branded Gangsters", the article went on to so say, that people were too scared to walk along the 200-yard stretch. Residents said that they were forced to walk on the other side of the road. Some of the kids' parents who lived on this street, stood up for us against the press and told them that we had nowhere to go. There were no youth clubs unless we travelled to the other side of Croydon where the nearest one was. One dad was quoted as saying" that the person who complained about us, probably didn't like children".

One of the dad's decided to set up a football team for us; Coburg Juniors FC, we were a Sunday league outfit who were part of the senior team "Coburg Utd" who played in a local league and were managed by him. I played for only one season with my dad as the manager of the juniors due to some indiscipline amongst some of the "prima donna's" dad was sacked, and we both left the club.

At school I was always bunking off, never completing my homework. I hated school, I didn't like the place or some of the teachers that taught me. I was always in trouble for silly things and I was also often in trouble with my parents too. When I was at Selhurst High, during one winter, there was a massive snowball fight with the girl's school next door, I decided to take it to the next level, and do an ambush with some of my friends. The school assembly hall had a balcony overlooking the hall which also doubled as the P.E gymnasium and was shared by both the boys and girls. We waited on the balcony when a group of girls came into the hall below, we let fire with snowballs which we brought in, unfortunately, someone who got hit said, they were hit with a stone? I have no idea who threw it. We were seen and reported. As none of us owned up we were given 2 weeks detention and a letter was sent home to our parents' house, it was a good job we didn't have a phone back then; I always got in before mum and dad so I intercepted the letter and binned it. I think I told them about it many years later.

My dad's side of the family were all heavy drinkers and gamblers, my dad had 15 siblings; two of them lived close by, they had nephews who were all in their twenties or thirties; whenever they got together, which was most weekends at one's house or another there was always a party. All us kids were in one room, the women cooking in the kitchen and my dad and his brothers and nephews with a couple of bottles of whiskey playing 3 card brag or poker.

At one of these sessions, there was a lot of booze around, my cousin and I decided it would be funny to piss in a bottle of orange juice and leave it on the drinks table! All hell broke out when the girlfriend of a nephew poured orange juice into her drink and sipped it.

When I was about 11 years old, Peter Broughton one of my school friends and I were on our way home from school, we had noticed that for the last couple of days milk was on someone's doorstep, so we decided to help ourselves. We didn't realize that a police car was driving slowly past; he lifted us! My parents went berserk. My mum took me to the house that had the milk outside and made me buy a fresh bottle to take around and apologise. My mum knocked on the door and a man opened it; he was quite a large man who had both of his arms in plaster. He said he didn't realize that the milk was there and that he couldn't bend to pick it up anyway. So, mum made me take them all in for him and put them away.

Sometimes these incidents were not my fault, but somehow, I got the blame. Little Jeff as he was known, a family friend, wanted to buy my air rifle off me. Without my parents knowing, I sold it to him, and within one day Jeff had shot some kid in the head from his bedroom window, again somehow it was my fault. When we were about 14, a friend asked me if I wanted to join the Air Training Corp (ATC), he told me that he was playing football for the wing and said I would get in easily.

I was very excited about this for 2 reasons, I always liked things to do with the military, always loved listening to my dad's stories of when he was in the Indian Army and I knew I would be able to play football; if I say so myself I wasn't a bad goalkeeper.

I joined the 97 Squadron ATC in Croydon and loved it. I loved drill and the range, Nijmegen march, and even had a few goes flying the Kirby Cadet glider. I eventually had a trial for the wing football team, but they already had a really good goalkeeper, so I tried out as a defender instead, I scored on my debut; an own goal and I didn't represent them again. I went on to have 2 great years in the cadets which ultimately lead to my career in the Royal Air Force.

One day I decided to visit our local careers' office in Norbury, South London to ask about the RAF. They took my details and told me to come back just before my 16th birthday and they sent me on my way, I was about 15 at the time.

It was now January 1979, I just returned to school after the school Christmas holidays ready to start my mock exams; when I got home one evening, my mum handed me a big brown envelope with my name and address printed on the front. I knew what it was straight away, I suppose the RAF roundels printed on the envelope gave it away! I quickly tore it open to find a letter and brochures about the RAF and the recruitment process. I had to contact them to make an appointment to see the recruitment officer.

The next day I made an appointment and was given a date of 2nd February; I happened to have a revision day that day, so my dad booked a day off as I needed an adult to accompany me.

When the day finally arrived, we had to get the bus. In those days we didn't have a car, in fact, my dad couldn't drive so we had to rely on public transport.

The careers office was right by the bus stop set in the middle of some shops on the busy A23, about 8 miles south of central London. There was a big sign displaying the words Royal Air Force and pictures of RAF planes in the window. The door was open and we went straight in, we were the only ones in there except for the corporal (Cpl), a junior Non-Commissioned Officer (JNCO) sitting behind a desk, he was in uniform, the same that we wore at Air Cadets, light blue shirt under a blue "woolly-pully" with corporal rank slides neatly on his epaulets. Dark grey trousers and highly polished shoes.

It was a very wet and cold morning as I remember it, it was nice to get inside a warm office. After the initial introductions, my ID was checked by means of my passport and we settled down in the waiting room with a nice hot drink. We filled in all the relevant paperwork and gave it back to the corporal sitting behind his desk.

The office was quite informative, there were posters everywhere showing pictures of the different type of aircraft used by the Royal Air Force, on another wall was a poster showing the rank structure between all 3 services and the equivalent of each rank. If I was successful, my first rank would be Aircraftsmen (AC), then after trade training, depending on the trade, and on completion of trade training, I would become Leading Aircraftsman (LAC) or if in a Technical trade, a Junior Technician (JT).

A door at the back of the office opened and a young-looking lad around my age came out, he had a big smile on his face and was accompanied by an older man and a woman, probably his parents. They were followed by a man in his thirties in uniform with 3 stripes on each shoulder, this was the Sergeant (Sgt), a Senior Non-Commissioned Officer (SNCO), I was going to see next.

A few moments later the Corporal (Cpl) got off his chair and went into the back office carrying my file, he closed the door behind him. We didn't have to wait long, the door opened, and a voice called out "Mr Gregory please come in".

I followed my dad into the office, we were met by Sgt Haddow who introduced himself. We took a seat as instructed. The room was like a bank manager's office with graphs on the wall which I didn't understand. There were squadron plaques on the wall behind his desk, most likely of the units he served in. There was also a boxing winners' trophy on his desk which he proudly showed off.

"If you are successful and you like sport, which I saw in your application form, you, could represent the RAF; there are any many sports that the RAF do". My dad just smiled, as he knew what that meant, as he was a boxer within the Indian Army and likewise his nephew, currently serving with the British Army on the Rhine in West Germany, was the British Army champion at the time.

The sergeant proceeded to go through the forms in my file, then told me that I had to sit an aptitude test. I was led into another room and given the test paper and a pen.

From what I remember some of the questions were simple to understand and there were some English and Maths questions too.

I handed the test sheet back to the Corporal who took me back into the room where the Sergeant and my dad were enjoying a cuppa and some military banter, mainly about the forces.

Sgt Haddow took the test sheet, marked it then said, "well done" and wrote something on my application form.

On the application form one of the questions was "Which Trade did I want to apply for"? With so many to choose from I picked Carpenter as my first choice, Aircraft Spray Painter as my second and Police as the third.

I suppose my choices derived from the fact that at school I was studying carpentry which I was quite good at; at home, I spent many days helping my dad around the house making and repairing things. We once built a "built-in bookshelf" into the chimney breast in the lounge. As for the painting, during the previous summer working at my dad's factory in the paint shop. I learned how to prepare surfaces, prime, and apply the first coat on the cases for the old public payphones and the yellow peril phones that used to be in some hotels and train stations. I was planning on returning there to work after my exams in the spring. As for my third choice, I have no idea what I was thinking.

Sgt Haddow then said that with the scores I got in my test, I would make a good Supplier. I must admit I had no idea what this meant. He showed me a picture of a sun-tanned airman wearing sunglasses refuelling a fighter jet. In the distance was a mountain surrounded by water glistening in the sunlight and beautiful trees. A very scenic picture. It was probably taken somewhere in Cyprus or Gibraltar where I knew there were RAF bases.

The Sgt said that I would be able to get a posting to these places once I got to my parent unit after training.

This was sold to me, but little did I know!

I signed as accepting the trade choice of Supplier and after a little discussion, I settled for 6-year fixed engagement with an option for 9. As I still had to complete my exams and I also had another commitment with the Air Cadets it was recommended that I enlist at the end of August or the beginning of September.

Whilst writing this story and reminiscing back I used a photocopy of my original application form which I acquired after I left the services. The following are some of the extracts:

"Aged 16 and 2 months of Indian extraction but not of upbringing. Neatly dressed in "Teddy Boy" style, drainpipes, and winkle picker shoes. Hair neatly groomed in that style. Relaxed and confident in manner and bearing. Very good powers of speech and expression. South London accent.

A proof that first impressions are no guide, this well mannered and mature young man with a lot of well-founded confidence in himself".

The interview discussions contained discussions around the school and the Air Training Corps. The Sgt wrote, " *I was amused that one of the reasons for joining was to get out of the rain, as we were not allowed inside at school".*

The headteacher wrote in his reference about me *"That I was a boy whose appearance gave the wrong impression.* The interviewer went on to say *"How I endorse that statement. I expected a different interview with guttural grunts for answers and a candidate with no depth at all. On the contrary, I interviewed a young man of 16 years who all the time appeared to be far older and mature for his age"*

The OIC concluded in his handwritten report *"Mr Gregory is a likeable but mature young man, with a ready smile and a passing resemblance to Mike Jagger"*

CHAPTER 2

Training and Beyond

I returned to school and could not wait to tell everyone that I was joining the Royal Air Force. Only now did I settle down in school, a bit too late really. I continued with my revision and finished off my woodwork project which was 2 bedside cabinets that were still standing until only recently.

As part of the process of leaving school I had to have careers meeting with my Year Head, he told me that I would never make it in the military as I was lazy and insubordinate.

The next couple of months went by quickly, I sat my exams and then I left school in June. After spending a few weeks back at work with my dad, painting public telephones to go in phone boxes, I was starting to get used to working and earning a wage, I was on £25 per week, but to me, that was a fortune, and I had no bills to pay.

In July in what would be my last time in Air Training Corps uniform I went to Holland with my Squadron for the Nijmegen marches. This event takes place every year and involves Armed Forces and cadets from all over Europe. It is a 4 day march which was originally a training march for the Dutch Infantry and pre-dates both the World Wars; but for us it was to commemorate the Battle of Arnhem.

After I arrived back home from Holland, there was a letter for me from the RAF. This contained my confirmation letter and joining instruction for a date of 19 September, but before this, I had to attend my Attestation, this would be in London on the 18th.

We had to go to an office near Whitehall, London to take the Oath and Swear Allegiance to Her Majesty the Queen.

The Oath read:

"I, Darrel Noel Joseph Gregory, Swear by Almighty God that I will be Faithfull and bear True Allegiance to Her Majesty Queen Elizabeth II, her Heirs and Successors and that I will, as Duty Bound, Honestly and Faithfully Defend Her Majesty and Successors, in Person, Crown, and Dignity against all Enemies and will Observe and Obey all Orders of Her Majesty, her Heirs and Successors, and of the Air Officers and other Officers set over me"

There were about 20 of us from all around London for the Attestation, we signed on the dotted line and were given our train warrants, which would allow us free travel up to RAF Swinderby the following day and we were also given the "Queens Shilling" this is a historical slang term referring to the earnest payment of one shilling given to recruits of the Armed Forces of the 18th and 19th century. [Source: Wikipedia].

Everyone hit it off with each other and formed little groups depending on which part of London we were from. I seemed to be drawn to a guy called Charlie, he too was from an Anglo-Indian family who lived over Wandsworth and another guy slightly older whose name I have forgotten. The three of us made arrangements to meet up at Waterloo station the next day, ready for our onward journey up to Lincolnshire. We said our goodbyes and I returned home to Croydon.

I don't think I got much sleep, but the day had finally arrived: 19th September 1979 will forever be embossed on my brain, a bit like riding a bike, I will never forget it. With all the essentials packed into a couple of suitcases and me suited and booted I was ready to go.

We arrived at Waterloo station with plenty of time to spare. My mum, dad, and Imelda came to see me off. Others were arriving too, I recognized some of them from the attestation the day before but there were more this time. All you could hear were different accents from all over the country, I never actually thought there would be this many. All were very smartly dressed in suits and their families were helping them with their luggage. I saw Charlie with his dad, they both came over to meet my family. After a bit of a chat we all said our goodbyes, I gave Imelda a kiss and hug, then my dad slung me a few £20 notes to help keep me going, my mum just sobbed and was being consoled by Imelda.

We picked up our cases and then went straight to the platform and produced our rail warrants before boarding the train.

"Next stop – Newark" came the announcement from the train's tannoy. We all got up and started to collect our belongings. It wasn't long before we were on the platform and the train set off into the distance. There were 2 or 3 airmen in uniform ushering us into some sort of order so they could do a roll call before we climbed upon the RAF bus for our final destination.

The bus was green and had a big yellow stripe down both sides with blue wording ROYAL AIR FORCE, it was very old probably from the 1950s or 60s and not too dissimilar to the ones you would see depicted in old black and white comedy films starring the likes of Sid James or Lesley Philips.

We arrived at the main gates of RAF Swinderby, the RAF School of Recruit Training. The school was once an operational bomber base transferred to Lincolnshire in 1971 from RAF Bridgenorth in Shropshire, this would home for the next 6 weeks.

The bus went straight through and pulled up outside a building. Our names were called out one at a time and we climbed down the step and onto the road, meanwhile, our luggage and cases were being offloaded onto the grass behind the bus.

We were lined up and we received our first order from one of the Drill Instructors (DI) "Flight Attennnsion". With a sharp not so synchronized manoeuvre we snapped our heals together, arms by our sides, stomach in, chest out, looking damn smart or at least we thought so. The DIs were all experienced NCOs from all trades within the RAF, some had been doing this for years, and it showed. They were experienced at making and breaking recruits to make them work as a team; this was done by using Dislocation of Expectation!

When we arrived at Swinderby we were all individuals. By the time we left, we would be operating as a unit and functioning as a team. We used to think that the DI's hated us all, but that was far from the truth.

They were pushing us to the limits, breaking us down then rebuilding us. We would get shouted at, some more than others, this is because they found it harder.

The idea was that the rest of the recruits would feel empathy for them, and start hating the DI's, we all would help each other, then start to work as a team.

The NCOs would all meet and discuss strategies, then we would compete against each other. When one flight did better, the other would get a bollocking, this would create a competitive streek and spurn you on to beat the others. They only had six weeks to turn us into confident young men.

Those of us who had been in the cadets prior stood out from the rest and the corporal acknowledged this, "you can see who's done this before, one of you may end up as senior man". We were turned into line and marched off to what was to be our accommodation for the next 6 weeks – Cheshire Block.

All military units' accommodation blocks are usually named after Soldiers, Sailors, or Airmen who were of military standing at their unit, regiment, or ship. Cheshire block was no different it was named after Lord Leonard Cheshire a World War 2 pilot who reached the rank of Group Captain and served from 1937-1946. A highly decorated officer of the highest calibre he was a holder of the Victoria Cross, Distinguished Flying Cross, and was mentioned in despatches a couple of times too.

Lord Cheshire was married to Sue Ryder who was a member of the Special Operations (Ops) Executive, she established Sue Ryder Care and later the Bouverie Foundation.

16 Flight

There were 60 of us on 16 Flight we were sent upstairs into Cheshire Block and split into 4 dorms, 15 in each. We picked our bedspace or pit as we called it, trying to be alongside someone that we already knew, the cliques were starting to form. Each dorm had 15 beds, 15 wardrobes, and 15 bedside units. The floor was highly polished, and all the walls were painted white. At the entrance to the room were a cleaning cupboard and a single room used as an office by the DI's. Going out of the door into the corridor there were the ablutions and cleaning cupboards, this then led into the opposite dorm. On the wall was a noticeboard this we would learn to look at every time we went past it. All our instructions for the day are neatly typed on A4 paper and pinned to it. Our names and room numbers were also typed out.
There was a copy of SRO's (Station Routine Orders) and SSO's (Station Standing Orders). A map of the station showing all the important amenities like the Junior Ranks (JR) mess which is used by all ranks below Cpl and the NAAFI (Navy, Army and Air Forces Institute) which was a social club and bar.

Back in the room, each bedspace had a wardrobe on one side and a small bedside cabinet on the other. The wardrobe which had a double door with a slot for a small padlock; on opening there was room on the right to hang clothes, and on the left a few shelves and a lockable compartment, on the inside of the door was a grey tray and rack that was used to hang your belts and service tie on. We unpacked our suitcase and bags and put our clothes neatly into our lockers. Little was I to know that I wouldn't be wearing any of these for the foreseeable future. We then had to collect and sign for our bedding which consisted of 2 white crisp sheets, 2 pillowcases, 2 white blankets, 1 grey blanket, and an orange bedspread; not like the duvets issued nowadays.

We were no longer allowed to walk anywhere, whenever we moved around the barracks, we "marched". So off we went trying to march with all our bedding in our arms back to Cheshire block.

The next morning, we formed up outside in 3s and were marched to the airman's mess where we had our first cooked breakfast, before being marched over to queue up at the camp barbers.

My hair was greased back, with a small quiff and a Duck's Arse or more commonly known as a DA on the back, combed back around the sides with a centre parting down the middle of the back of the head. This hairstyle originated back to the 50s and 60s and was quite still the fashion for some in the late 70s.

My turn came around and I sat in the chair, there were 2 or 3 barbers cutting hair all wearing dust coats looking very uniformly: there was a poster next to the mirror in front saying "BE SMART keep within limits" and a slogan underneath "The hair of the head is to be cut and trimmed". Extract from The Queens Regulations for the Royal Air Force. I was asked how I wanted my hair, my description of what I wanted and what I received were two different things, we all went in looking different but came out looking the same.

The training we were about to embark on was six weeks long, of which you were expected to pass a series of tests and courses.

The most exciting thing so far was about to happen – a trip to clothing stores to collect the mountains of equipment and clothing that we were going to need for the next 6 weeks and beyond.

Uniform:
· Beret Standard Air Force blue/grey with RAF badge
· 4 Light blue shirts cotton material
· 2 Dark blue shirts denim material
· 2 Grey overalls
· Safety boots (ankle high with steel toe caps)
· 2 Pairs of grey trouser (same as the ambulance service and the RAC).
· Woolley pulley round neck with elbow patches
· "Thunderbird" jacket zip up the from and 2 pockets on the side
· Rain Mac "flasher mac"
· 2 pairs of shoe's Oxfords with toe cap

· 2 black ties
· Trouser belt woven denim with brass buckle
· 1 pair of steel toe cap boots ankle-high
· No. 1 Uniform (fitted), to be collected at a later date ready for passing out parade should I make it!
· No. 1 Hat
· 1 Blue PE shirt
· 1 White PE shirt
· 2 pairs of denim colour knee-length PE shorts
· 1 Pair white plimsoles

Combats:
· Helmet and camouflage cover
· 1 pair of DMS boots
· Combat trousers
· Combat jacket
· Green woolly pulley
· Woolley gloves
· Camouflage cap peaked
· Neck scarf netted
· Putties
· Blue kit bag
· 56 pattern webbing, back-pack ammo pouch, kidney pouch, and water bottle pouch
· Sleeping Bag "Maggot"
· Bedroll
· Mess tins one inside the other
· KFS (Knife, Fork, and Spoon)

· Water bottle black with mug and connector for S6 gas mask
· S6 Gas Mask
· Spare S6 canister and decontamination kits
· Weapon cleaning kit for SLR
· 2 out of date NBC suits for training purposes
· Tin cup
· Drill rifle (dummy SLR)

This was just some of the initial kit recruits would find themselves signing for, some of it would be given back at the end of the 6 weeks, the rest we kept. This kit is now my property if I lose it, I pay for it – simple! Later in our careers, we would find ways of accumulating various bits of kit, the shinier the better.

We took it all back to ·our pits in Cheshire block and carefully put it away, whilst some were running around the room wearing their helmets others including myself were preparing our kit. We would spend the next day or so, learning how to care for and maintain it, we were shown how to iron a shirt and press the trousers, we were given tips on how to "bull" our shoes and boots, to inspection standard. A few of us already had some practice in the cadets and were able to pass on our wisdom to the other recruits. During the war and national service most then would use spit and polish as a combination. I only used parade gloss Kiwi polish and a soft yellow cloth, I never used spit or cotton wool.

We were taught about service life in the RAF. We learned about the customs and traditions, as well as the history and were given our service numbers and had to recite this over and over again. For most of us, our first taste of basic first aid and what to do during a nuclear attack.

Bull Night or Domestic Duties Evening

Every Monday evening cleaning jobs would be allocated, usually, you would work in teams of 2 or 3 to clean every part of the block.

Usually just wearing a pair of shorts and old trainers. Using Glitto scouring powder and scouring pads you would get on your hands and knees and scrub every part of the shower floor and tiles, every bit of porcelain and Brasso or Duraglit brass and metal polish on every tap and plug hole. The vinyl floors would be swept and the highly polished using a buffer (Buffer a long wooden pole attached to a weight and a blanket underneath you would swing this thing from left to right and back again along the floor to get it shinning) these were few and far between and to be shared by the whole block. If you were on toilet cleaning duty you would try your hardest to stop anyone from using them after. After a particular bull night, in the morning, someone had done the biggest shit you have ever seen, blocking one of the toilets. Luckily, it was someone from the room opposite; they held a "kangaroo court" with one of the recruits who were notorious for being a right reasty git who was always unclean and never showered. He was made to clean the toilet and flush the turd. I heard he was dunked into a bath and scrubbed with a bass broom after the inspection.

As soon as you had finished your task you would then proceed to do your pits and then finally you get your kit ready for inspection in the morning.

Everyone would be up and out of their pits extra early as there was still one thing left to do.

Bed Packs

There was an art to making the ideal bed pack ready for room inspection, though there are a few versions, from memory it consisted of all the blankets and 2 sheets folded in a certain way so you could not see the edges, these were to the exact same size as the others.
Grey blanket first then a sheet laid on top followed by the white blanket, then the other sheet then the 2nd grey blanket. This would be carefully lined up and best with the help of a buddy you would wrap the bedspread around the blankets and tuck in very tight. This would be carefully placed on the bed at the head end. The 2 pillows would be placed on top. Some recruits put theirs together the night before and slept next to the bed in their maggots.

26

Room Inspection

Standing at ease in front of your bed, dressed in the order of the day depending on what was on the timetable to follow. If its PT then you would be in your PT kit, drill in number 2s, GDT in combats. All your kit is laid out on the bed, everyone's looking the same. Shirts neatly folded and all the same size, shoes highly bulled and looking like mirrors.

Total silence waiting for the flight commander to turn up. "Room, room attention" bellows from the door, then in walks Flight Commander and his entourage. All the recruits standing firm, arms tucked into their sides, heels together, chin up chest out. As they walk in front of each recruit staring straight into the eyes, "Name Rank and Number" one of the NCOs would shout, the service number would be shouted back followed "Aircraftsman DN Gregory, Sir" In the early days of recruit training, the DI's would always find things wrong with your own your kit, even if it is perfect, and when they do you would be punished for it; "down and give me 20" they would say or the would make you run around the block or extra give extra drill. One occasion a few of us had been picked up so the whole flight was sent running, out of the room down the stairs, onto the grass around the block and back again – repeat. We would be laughing whilst coughing and spitting out phlegm whilst other blocks are doing the same thing. Then returning to the room and finding all the beds turned over and everyone's kit mixed up. "Wankers"!

I marched into their office halted and stood to attention "you asked to see me Sgt" I said; if you are in the presence of different ranks, and you addressed them you always used the highest rank in the room, Sgt Prince out ranked Cpl Tucker. Where is your weapon Gregory?" a quick simple answer is "It's in my locker Sgt" I confidently replied! As you never left your weapon unattended unless it is locked away and as the weapons were only specially adapted drill weapons, old unused Enfield .303 which have been decommissioned with all the working parts removed and the barrel sealed up, they could be locked in your locker. Cpl Tucker then said, "I suggest you go and get it then". Puzzled, as I wondered why I was asked this and no one else. I went back to my room to find my locker doors open and the padlock open hanging on the door.

The contents of my locker was everywhere, my kit scattered all over everyone else's beds in the room. Everything was opened, my wash kit was everywhere, socks unrolled, and thrown on top of someone else's locker.

In those days I used to smoke. I had an unopened box of 200 Benson and Hedges; this was now open and some of the packets opened and thrown everywhere. I gathered everything up quickly and dumped it all back in my locker making sure that I locked the padlock this time. My weapon was not there. Shitting myself, I went back to their office and they were sitting there with my weapon and smoking some of my fags. I learned a valuable lesson that day.

<u>P.E</u>

Physical fitness played a big part in the military, if you are unfit physically. Then you are unfit to fight. Regular PT (most days), would include gym work, climbing the wall bars, ropes, indoor and outdoor assault courses, and the dreaded BFT runs, which required you to run 1.5 miles within a certain time depending on your age. Quite often when we moved from one place to another in PT kit, we would have to run in step and not march. There was always competition to see who the best flight was, the rivalry was fierce. PE also included competitive sports.

<u>Ground Defence Training (GDT)</u>

The RAF Regiment plays a big role in the defence of the RAF airfields at home and abroad, some are lucky enough (or not) to become GDT instructors where they get to teach us some aspects of their trade. GDT was taught at RAF Swinderby by a flight of RAF Regiment NCOS or Rock Apes as they are known by all branches of the armed services, this is due to their escapades on the Rock of Gibraltar. GDT will be an ongoing annual event when we get posted to our new units, this course will teach us the basics.

One of the most exciting bits of training were the exercises, we would be fully kitted out in all our combats carrying our dummy weapons. Shipped out on the green bus and sent to some woodland somewhere in the Lincolnshire countryside. We would be sleeping out in tents and we were shown some basic fieldcraft skills. We would be shown how to use camouflage effectively, how to "dig in" and most importantly how to eat.

This would be our first taste of field rations. A 24-hour ration pack which has enough food to last for the whole day and consisted of tea, coffee and dried milk powder, some biscuits and toilet paper; very similar to pieces of tracing paper used in school, a tin of stew, curry or babies head and bacon grill for breakfast and a packet of Spangles. You also got with a book of matches and hexamine blocks and stove for heating it.

Toilets in the field were usually a bucket in the woods filled with a chemical called Racasan for us to shit in, this would be emptied into a hole dug in the ground and burned. However, for training purposes, there was a brick building nearby for our ablutions.

Weapon handling skills were taught, which included stripping the weapon down, cleaning it and putting it back together again, then doing it again, and again. By the end of 6 weeks, you could do it blindfolded.

The L1A1 Self-Loading Rifle was a British Version of the Belgium FN Rifle. Introduced to the British Forces in 1954, it weighed 9.5lbs (empty) was 45" long and was a gas operated semi-automatic weapon firing 7.62 mm rounds.

Whenever you pick up a weapon the first thing you do is to carry out a safety check. Remove the magazine, tilt the weapon to the right and cock the weapon 3 times with your left hand, if there are any rounds ejected they will land on the floor and not hit you in the face; you then pull back the cocking handle once more and lock it back, you look into the breach to make sure there are no rounds in the chamber, give it a shake and put your index finger in to check and remove it. Release the cocking handle and let the breach block and slide go forward by itself. Undo the safety catch, fire-off the action and place the safety catch back to safe.

Once you have the weapon, there are some golden rules.
· Never leave it unattended, you may have to sleep with it

· Never lean the weapon against anything always lie it down on the floor, cocking handle facing upwards.
· Keep it clean at all times
· When handing it over to someone, always carry out a safety check; when you hand it over, pass it with the breach still open butt first so the person receiving can see if it clear they will take it off you and release the working parts and fire off the action.

The Range

Firing from the prone position, sitting, and standing positions. We would usually fire off 5 rounds lying down, the target would be checked and the sites on the rifle adjusted (zeroing). Once adjusted you would be given orders on the range to take up a position and given an order "Five rounds at the target in front carry-on". You would take aim and fire off the required rounds.
Stoppages

"Weapon fires – weapon stops" shouts the instructor. Immediately you apply the safety catch, 'cock, hook and look' open the chamber and await further instructions as to what was supposed to have caused the stoppage. "Rounds in the magazine rounds in the chamber" you would release the working parts forward and carry on firing. The same instruction is said again, we would follow the same immediate action drill, this could mean the gas regulator would need adjusting, "Rounds in the magazine rounds in the chamber" apply safety, release the working parts forward. Bring the weapon down to your side and adjust the gas regulator and then carry on firing. Weapon fires weapon stops again, no rounds in the magazine no rounds in the chamber. You would carry out the same drill, but with the working parts locked open, you would eject the empty magazine and replace it with a full one, release the working parts and continue firing at the target.

Theses drills are practised over and over again and can still be recited over 40 years later. Dependent on the type of weapon you are training on the drills may differ.

Once completed all the empty brass cases would be collected. We would then stand in line carry out the safety check and leaving the chamber open for the senior person on the range to inspect the weapon, as he approached each person from behind he would tap you on the shoulder, look into the chamber and shout clear, in a snap you would release the cocking handle, undo the safety fire off the action and return to safety catch to safe. Next would be the declaration, in turn, and as loud as possible "I have no live rounds or empty cases in my possession Sgt or whichever rank he was.

Gas Gas Gas

Extract from "The 1983 Survive to Fight Aide Memoire" which was issued to every serviceman "The threat that NBC weapons will be used in war is very real. Provided you are skilled in using your NBC Individual Protection Equipment (IPE) it will protect you from the hazards from these weapons. During military training, you will be taught and practised in the various individual drills associated with operating in NBC IPE.

If you are to survive an NBC attack, you have to be highly proficient in the survival drills. The skill at performing these drills is not something you can develop when a war starts. Constant practice is needed.

There are 21 Tasks in the Survive To Fight Manual ranging from recognizing all the equipment and wearing it,the chemical Immediate Action Drill (IAD) and decontamination.; with everything else in between.

On hearing the shout "gas gas gas", the IAD drill will kick in, you would take a big breath hold it, close your eyes as tight as you can, whilst removing your S6 Respirator from its pouch and put it on and tighten the strap whilst making sure that it was a good fit, and put up your hood and tighten at the chin. You would then expel the breath you were holding by shouting "gas gas gas" this is to expel the air in your lungs, you could then open your eyes and adjust. All that had to be done within 9 seconds. "Mask In Five – Survive, Mask In Nine – Just in Time"

The drill was to give protection against Nuclear, Biological, and Chemical (NBC) attack. The full Noddy suit consisted of trousers, smock (Hoodie), over boots, inner gloves, outer rubber gloves, plus decontamination kit consisting of Fullers Earth powder and blot bangs. Trouser on first, 2 straps on each leg to be tightened up there were two long straps at the back, you would cross them at the back bring over your shoulder cross them on your chest and tie them to the top of the trousers, then the smock is put on and straps on the sides and wrists, to ensure no gases can get in. The over boots would then be put on, on top of your footwear, then the cotton inner gloves, and finally the outer gloves. This was all well in good in the winter as it kept you warm, in the summer you would sweat like a diabetic in a cake shop!

With the NBC suit on and the respirator neatly packed into the pouch around your waist we were lead into the gas chamber; a small brick building the size of a double garage, with no windows a concrete floor, and a roof and a table made of bricks right in the centre. The door would be closed and the instructor would light a small white tablet on the brick table, there would be at first a small stream of smoke coming off the tablet, then within a few seconds the smoke would fill the room. We were already starting to feel the effects of CS Gas, this was to be our first of many gas chamber experiences. CS gas is now in the room and the instructor would shout "Gas Gas Gas", we were starting to cough now as we're unable to hold our breaths much longer, but still had to endure at least 9 seconds whilst we try and locate our respirators. A drill which we practised on numerous occasions outside of the gas chamber or in the block, some of the lads in competition which each other to see if they could crack it in less time than his 'oppo' (a military term for friend or buddy). In reality, the first time we would be lucky to do it in under 20 seconds, probably longer! With our respirators finally in place and breath expelled, we would do a quick buddy-buddy check with the person next to you, making sure that they are completely covered, no stray hairs under the seals and no skin showing.

One at a time when the instructor tapped you on the shoulder, you would remove your S6 and shout out your name, rank and service number, he may say run around the table or start asking you stupid questions, just to make you talk; it is hilarious watching everyone doing this until it's your turn!. By this time you have breathed out what little oxygen you had left in your lungs and then you breathe in CS gas; your chest is hurting your face is stinging and you just want to get out of there. One at a time the door will open, and another recruit just falls out into the welcome fresh air.

At the time of training, this type of chemical warfare was only a threat but still needed to be practised. In a real chemical environment, you would need to eat, drink and shit too at some stage, you could be in your NBC suits for days or even weeks at a time. To do any of these tasks you would need to decontaminate first using the fullers earth, wipe it on your gloves, bang it and then rub it in or blot - bang – rub as it is known in the military. Once your gloves were done then the outside of the S6 would be decontaminated to eat or drink or your waistband for ablutions! To drink or eat, take a deep breath, close your eyes, open the S6 place food or water in the mouth, put S6 back breath out the swallow – repeat. As for the defecation drills, I'll just leave that to the readers' imagination.

Drill

Drill training took place every day, either by just marching between destinations on the base or on the parade square.

The parade square is said to be sacred ground. After the battle when the retreat was sounded and the unit had re-assembled for a roll call and count the dead, a hollow square was formed. The dead were placed within the square and no one used the area as a thoroughfare. Now the parade ground represents this square and hence a unit's dead. It is considered hallowed ground soaked with the blood of our fallen and the area is respected as such.

Drill is an important aspect of military training, it teaches teamwork, discipline, and how to take orders quickly, which will help you on the battlefield.

As a former Cpl in the Air Training Corps, I was used to doing drill and quite good at it as I had represented my ATC squadron at 2 drill competitions during my short time there. Indeed, a couple of times I was asked by Cpl Tucker to stand in and give some drill orders whilst he went for a smoke break.

Passing Out Parade

The passing out parade is the ultimate goal. You've made it, you have passed basic training. You get to see your family again, as during the 6 weeks we were only allowed 1 weekend at home, and then you were still in uniform as you were not allowed to travel in civvies.

On the morning of the Passing Out Parade, we were all up early, most of our kit was neatly packed away into our kit bags, except for our Number One uniforms which were hanging neatly on our locker doors, our hats were sitting proudly on the bed packs and our shoes highly polished (bulled) looking like mirrors on the toe caps. To the mess early for our last fry up and then back to Cheshire block to get changed into our number ones ready for the final march past and salute.

It didn't matter that it was pissing down and cold, as the adrenaline kicked in once the parade had started. In ranks of 3, at open order, we were inspected and then marched around the parade square and the Station Commander took the salute as we all gave an eye's right.

At this time there was a break in the weather and the sun started to come through the clouds so the final part of the parade can still take place - the famous Fly Past. A lone Vulcan bomber from nearby RAF Coningsby flew low over the parade ground with its loud engines roaring and into the distance until it could no longer be heard. Silence is all around then the final salute and dismiss as the parade came to a close. No longer a recruit, but an Aircraftsman.

Watching in the pouring rain was my mum and dad and my future wife Imelda. At one point when it was raining Imelda had to stop my mum from bringing an umbrella onto the parade square for me. Must have something to do with me not liking being in the rain.

After spending one week at home on annual leave, the whole of 16 Flight was sent to RAF Uxbridge in Middlesex to train for the Festival of Remembrance at the Royal Albert Hall. We spent one week learning how to march downstairs with a live military band; in this case, it was the band of the Royal Marines. This was a proud moment early in my new career.

RAF Uxbridge on outskirts of Middlesex was the home of The Queens Colour Squadron (QCS) RAF Regiment; their primary role was to provide ceremonial duties and to escort the colour as well as protection of RAF bases around the world.

As recruits who had just finished basic training we were best placed to take on the duty at the Festival of Remembrance and it also looked good for public relations to show young enthusiastic airmen straight out of basic training marching with the likes of the QCS, Royal Marines and Chelsea pensioners amongst contingents from all the armed services and cadet forces. We put 2 shows on that day, the evening performance was in front of HM The Queen.

Once this duty came to an end it was time to say our goodbyes. A few dozen lads from all walks of life, now brothers in arms who all went through basic training together. Some we may bump into again further into our careers, some, in fact, most we probably would never see or hear from again. But if we did it would be like we never had been apart; this is a fact that we would encounter later in our military careers.

RAF Hereford was built on Credenhill, Herefordshire in 1939 and in-use with the RAF from 1940 – 1994. Predominantly used as a training establishment for many RAF trades, including, Suppliers, Cooks and Admin staff. In 1994, the base was handed over to the Special Air Service (SAS), to use as its main HQ after the closure of Sterling Lines, which was just down the road in Hereford.

For the next 7 weeks, we would be cooped in classrooms for lectures and practical exercises to learn the trade of Supplier. The classrooms were old wooden Nissan huts all in lines at the back of the parade square.

he parade square itself was no different to the ones at Swinderby or Uxbridge, the only difference was this one had a "Gate Guard" a solemn camouflaged Spitfire!

We still had to maintain our fitness, discipline, drill and GDT including another go in a gas chamber, after all, we were still in training. As we were no longer recruits, had the privilege of wearing green slides on our epaulettes. We all held the rank of AC (Aircraftman) except for one airman who was training to be a cook he was already a Senior Aircraftsmen (SAC), a rank that is not usually achieved until at least 1 year as a Leading Aircraftsman (LAC) which is the rank that we will leave RAF Hereford with if we pass the course. He was also on 16 Flight with me and we found out later that he was already a qualified chef and was previously in the Army but was discharged on medical grounds.

To be honest, I found trade training to be a bit boring, I had no real interest in becoming a Supplier, as it was not a trade I chose. In fact, during my whole career, I never got many choices but had to endure the seven weeks to be able to get to my first unit. After about the 3rd week it was "choice time again" we would be given the chance to apply for our first unit. Being a London boy, my first choice was RAF Stanmore, second was RAF West Drayton both in London and my third was RAF Biggin Hill near to where Imelda and my parents lived in Croydon. I got RAF Odiham, a unit that I had never heard of, but others where envious as RAF Odiham was the main base for Northern Ireland turn around; any person from any of the 3 services who get posted to N.I. will fly from Odiham usually by Wessex or Puma helicopter. Anyone serving at

Odiham would also be given the chance to travel over during the troubles if they wanted to.

CHAPTER 3

Home of the Battlefield Helicopter

RAF Odiham (home of the battlefield helicopter) is situated in a small village not far from Basingstoke in Hampshire. During WW2, the base was used by North American Mustangs and Hawker Typhoons and just after the surrender in Europe the base was turned into a POW camp.

I arrived at Odiham quite late one evening in early January 1980, it was cold and the snow was starting to melt. I can't remember how I got to the unit from Hook railway station. I arrived at the Guardroom and was given my accommodation details.

Hastings Block, my new home, was named after the aircraft and also the battle in 1066. The building looked like it was built in 1066, I wouldn't be surprised if Harold stayed in one of the rooms. The rooms were set out exactly like Cheshire Block - H blocks. In each of the room, the bed spaces had two beds with a plasterboard partition at the sides and four of the standard used wardrobes across the bed spaces to create a room; there was a gap in between each block of 2 wardrobes to create a doorway. The rooms should have been condemned, not a nice thing to face on your first posting. The block was situated on the east side of the parade square, come car park. To the west was another block that looked the same as Hastings. On the south side was the Airman's Mess and the NAAFI, to the North was the main road through the camp with the aircraft hangars, workshops and Supply Squadron.

Behind the accommodation block on the west side stood other more modern accommodation blocks, each belonging to the different squadrons where eventually I would be given my own room. But in the meantime, I was stuck in this dump.

I had settled in well at my parent unit and was lucky to get the opportunity to work in different parts of the Supply Squadron. I was enjoying my first unit and in particular the camaraderie amongst everyone.

I used to travel back to Croydon at weekends but was getting fed up with trains, so I decided I wanted to get a car. I went and bought myself a 1968 Austin Mini from a guy that we knew in our local pub. I put on some "L" plates and used to drive it around at weekends, I looked like a genuine learner as I always had Imelda sitting in the front seat, little did anyone know, she didn't have a full licence either, but we got away with it.

I was eventually sent on a driving course to RAF St Athan just outside of Cardiff. I started the course on the Monday and was put forward for my driving test for the following week. Learning to drive in the military is different to learning to drive in civvy street. In the military you are taught to drive both defensively and offensively depending on the circumstances and road conditions as opposed to being taught just how to pass the test. After you have passed and been signed off by the MTO (motor Transport Officer) you could drive almost anything within the lower weight categories; but would still need to have a familiarisation test before you were loose with the vehicle.

I passed my test first time but had to do a "theory test" beforehand, something that wasn't introduced in the UK until 1996. Once I passed my test, the course wasn't over, I still had to do a night drive with a co-driver navigating and then swap over for the drive back to St Athan. The final day was defensive manoeuvres on the skid pan in a 4x4 Long Wheelbase Land Rover (LWB). I had only ever driven my Mini and the standard Ford Escort estate that I passed my test in. So, getting the opportunity to get in the driver's seat of the LWB was very exciting. The skid pan was on an area of the airfield that was used only for driver training, the walls of the pan were built with old tyres, so crashing into them wouldn't be a problem, though the idea was to control the vehicle in a skid and not crash. The LWB was adapted for use on the pan by putting a couple of badly worn tyres on it, not much H&S in those days.

I was first up, I climbed in and put on my seatbelt, started the engine into gear and go! Hurtling around the track as fast as possible, straight into an oil patch; and just to make it more difficult the instructor would spray a jet of water onto the oil using a fire hose then you would brake as hard as you can, get the LWB into a spin and try and take control of it.

That was now 2 vehicles on my FMT600, (military driving licence) for every vehicle that you drove it had to be signed off to be able to drive it.

Back at Odiham, my new job was on Forward Supply, most new drivers in supply got this job, basically driving equipment around to different areas on and off base. A few months down the line and we would be driving anything from the OC Supplies Mini to LWB, forklift trucks and Bedford lorries. One vehicle which was probably the oldest in the whole of the British forces was a 35CWT Bedford Hawson van, built in the 1950s, four-speed, though 1st gear didn't work at all, so 3 speed really. It was painted the standard NATO olive green, had more scratches and dents in than a banger racing car which had just finished 20 laps at Snetterton racetrack. It had a very high back that you could stand up in and was ideal for doing deliveries around the camp.

One cold rainy day, I was on a routine drop and had to reverse up to the side door of the ASF hangar (Aircraft Servicing Flight). There is an ASF at every RAF station that have aircraft, it is in these hangars that deeper repairs are carried out on different types of aircraft operated by the flying squadrons.

The side entrance of the hangar was wide enough for a car to drive into, but not something of this height, so I stopped just short of the top of the entrance. I did the drop, climbed into the back of the vehicle and closed the tailgate behind me, I walked through the back and climbed into the driver's seat. I put on my seat belt, started the engine and selected 2nd gear, as 1st was not working. I pressed on the accelerator raised the clutch to get the bite as I was facing a slight uphill incline; I released the handbrake and pressed down hard on the accelerator to get some momentum going on the slope; Whoosh! before I could hit the brake the vehicle flew backwards and "wallop" I hit the top of the vehicle into the hangar. Had I parked a little up the slope, I would have been able to stop short, but I hadn't, all because I didn't want to get wet.

I had to get out in the rain and assess the damage, the roof was slightly rippled to the top corner and I broke the indicator housing, that was it. I could have gotten away with it, but the SEngO (Senior Engineering Officer) watched me do it, so I had no choice but to report the incident to the MT SNCO and completed the FMT 3 accident paperwork.

Eventually, all the paperwork went through and I was found to be in breach of SSOs (Station Standing Orders). SSOs clearly stated that when driving a service vehicle, you start off by selecting first gear.
I had gone to select 2nd but had accidentally found the reverse, which was to the left of 2nd gear. I was subsequently charged.

At the charge hearing, I was outside the boss's office dressed in my number two uniform but without my beret and standing to attention, at a charge, only the escort and the SNCO marching us in would wear their berets. The order was given by the SNCO "prisoner and escort by the centre quick march" and in when we marched. We were halted in front of the OC I said my name, rank and number and the charge was read out to me; shitting myself having never been on this side of a charge before, I had only ever been an escort a few times. I felt in like a criminal, a man on death row. I was found guilty of disobeying SSOs. I was asked the question that is always asked by the officer reading the charge "do you want to accept my punishment or have your case heard by Court Martial".

I took his punishment; I was fined £25 with £25 stoppages from pay.

They took the Hawson into the spray shop, straightened the slightly rippled roof, painted it NATO olive green and repaired the indicator. A few weeks later we were asked to return the Hawson to the MT flight and pick up a new

35CWT Bedford flatbed as the Hawson was being scrapped! Bastards, and I was still being skimmed of £50 from my next pay.

In 1981, I was called in to see my Flight Sergeant (FS), Mick Harber, he was probably one of the nicest FS I have ever worked with, he had been about and seen it all and was as fair as they come. He said to me that they needed

a supplier who could drive a 4 tonner to go on exercise with a 33 Squadron Pumas on Exercise Amber which was a big NATO exercise in Denmark which was to run simultaneously with another NATO exercise in Norway.

The idea for this exercise was to test the Pumas aircrew's capability against enemy forces in a colder climate than what they were used to. I would be only one of two suppliers going.

We were to drive to Harwich in convoy, board the SS Dana Anglia (DFDS ferry), dock in Esberg, then drive to Rinstaed and set up a defence base for the Pumas.

We set off early in the morning in convoy, with us in the lead vehicle with 9 or 10 military vehicles following. The convoy included other 4 tonners some pulling trailers and one with our 2 Norton Commando despatch motorbikes in the back and also LWB and SWB Land rovers carrying the troops, the rules of a convoy is that the slowest vehicle is always at the front, the lead and the rear vehicle had a coloured flag flying to signify the start and end of the convoy, no one is allowed to overtake. We had radio communications with the last vehicle and with "Stingray" the call sign for the boss, who was OC 33 Squadron.

I drove for the first part of the journey to Harwich with my oppo doing the navigating; the steering on these vehicles was heavy, and it didn't help with the amount of kit we were carrying. We had loaded enough mobility equipment for the entire squadron, including about 50 x 5-gallon water containers these were filled in the vehicle when we were doing the loading, we just got a hosepipe and filled each one up in the back of the vehicle. We also had cam-nets, and these specially built aluminium containers called Special Transit Containers (STC) which are used to transport delicate aircraft equipment like gyros, radar spares and navigation dials. Looking back, it probably wasn't very clever to have the aircraft spares and the water on the same vehicle, but I suppose as we're going to cross the North Sea if we sank it wouldn't matter anyway. The other vehicles were carrying personnel, vehicle spares, field kitchens and most importantly our rations or rat packs as they were known.

In the ration packs, there was enough food to last 24-hours, there were tins of chicken curry, bacon grill and 'babies heads' (steak and kidney pie), these had no crust on top hence looking like a baby's head; a trick that we told was to place a tin of food on the exhaust manifold before you started the journey. Under the side panel just above the wheel arch, the exhaust manifold is exposed and has ledges where the housing is bolted together, this area gets very hot after a while so we would place a tin snuggly in between the downpipes. I placed 2 tins of the Bacon Grill just before we departed, one for each of us. So, they would be nice and hot by the time we made our first stop in our scheduled layby.

When we arrived at our first stop off about 2 hours into the journey we would stretch our legs and a strategic pee in the woods, the side panels on the vehicles were all being opened, a very nice treat, the only problem was, you needed a good pair of gloves as the tins were the same temperature as the exhaust.

Our orders stated that we were not allowed to break convoy except in an emergency, so we could not use the service stations along the way. We continued the journey to Harwich and on arrival, our admin clerk and one of the SNCOs checked us all in with a customs officer who came to each vehicle for a passport check, most of us had NATO travel orders and the requirement for a passport into another European country wasn't always necessary. We locked up the vehicles and went to our bunks for the sea crossing, this would be the only time that we would get a hot civvy meal for the next 2 weeks. The sea trip was about 24 hours, with another 4 to 5-hour drive on the other side.

The site which we were to set up on and defend was a field on the outskirts of Ringstaed town. There were streets and houses in the distance and some shops and bars on the other side. At night you could hear men and women laughing as they came out of the bars having had a few Carlsberg's. We were not permitted unless on duty to leave the perimeter under any circumstances; doing so could mean that you would be charged resulting in getting 'jankers' (military punishment) or even put before a court-martial.

The field where we set up was once a farm and still had the farmhouse buildings and some stables all in good condition, these were used to set up our HQ, Ops room, communications centre, medical centre/field hospital and the armoury.

All our weapons were flown over in one of the Pumas as we were not allowed to carry them on our persons; we would be leaving British waters and it was peacetime.

We collected our weapons from the armoury and we would now be treating the exercise as if we were on operational duties.

The SLR 7.62 automatic rifle was the preferred weapon of choice for most of us and sometimes it was the only choice. The sub-machine gun (SMG) was issued to SNCOs and Officers only, the aircrew had 9mm Browning pistols and the RAF Regiment, their personal weapons were the SLR and some also carried the General Purpose Machine Guns (GPMG).

All of our vehicles and the 3 Puma Helicopters which had already landed ahead of us needed to be guarded 24/7, so the easiest way was to guard our own. We set up our camp beds in the back of the lorry near the cab and made it quite cosy, we then had the STC containers separating us from the spares at the rear which we made into our Mobility Supply Flight (MSF) store.

Crowds of children had already started gathering around trying to get a look at what we were doing. There had been a temporary perimeter fence erected by someone locally and only one entrance in and out, which was good as it meant fewer guards on duty. As well as our own duties of providing spares and arranging for new bits of kit to be brought in, we had to provide a defence.

Two men on a four on four off stag would guard the one entrance, the Rocks would set up GPMG posts at certain strategic positions and there was always a foot patrol going around.

Stand to at dawn and dusk, which was a pain in the arse having to set up defences around the perimeter (on the inside) and pretend that we may get attacked. Lying in the prone position watching your arc of fire, not allowed to eat, drink, smoke or fart in case we gave away our position to the enemy. Dawn and dusk were the most likely time that you could be attacked.

Every day the Pumas would disappear on some sort of mission (training exercise) and return, there would always be something wrong with one of them. The techies would do an AF/BF (after flight/before flight check) and service the helicopter if it were needed.

Food was usually good on an exercise. I didn't mind the compo, as you can add to it to make it more enjoyable, the only problem was having time to eat it after you had prepared it. The oatmeal blocks were a favourite and you could spread the sandwich paste on the biscuits AB (alternative bread or arse blocker).

At breakfast, you would pop a tin of breakfast bacon grill or compo sausages into a mess tin with some water and bring to the boil using a small stove with hexamine blocks. Once the food was heated sufficiently, you would use that mess tin of water to wash and you would make a tea or coffee with the other; tip! give your teeth a brush first then rinse and spit out using the brew, then eat your food, if you messed up when spitting you would have mint tea!

We also had the cooks on hand with their field kitchens for a more culinary field experience, still using compo rations but with added veg and fruit and if we were really lucky, they would knock up some fresh bread.

Clothing in the field is challenging, you have what you have in the field, what you are wearing and a spare set, and just the one pair of boots. Sometimes there's time and space to do your 'dobi' (slang word for laundry, derived from India) depending on the exercise, but in operational situations, that is completely different, more about that later.

"Stand To" is called and I take up position fully camouflaged with my face covered in "cam-cream". The idea of camouflage is to blend in with your surroundings in the hope that the enemy does not see you. I already know my arc of fire, as this would have been established when I was given my defensive position. I know the distances to certain points within my arc, a tree, a bush a distant church. An example would be If we spot any enemy movement within the arc, we should be able to call a "contact" on the radio.

"This is "*give call sign*"

"Contact Wait Out" this is the order for complete radio silence, everyone would be waiting for the next message.

"This is *call sign* 110 metres to the North, small white building to the left of the church person gone to ground on the right side over"

The next thing would be to wait for orders from the ops room unless we come under fire, only then would we return fire.

These sightings could be the enemy on a recce watching what we are doing, or it could be a civilian just going about their business. During exercises like this especially in foreign countries, it is usually the latter.

About halfway through the exercise during a dusk stand to, the silence was broken with the rattle of a GPMG firing short bursts not far from our position. You could see the flash from the weapon's muzzle but could not see where they were firing. The reason for this is that the weapons on exercise are all firing blank ammunition.

When using blank ammunition the weapon needs to have a BFA (Blank Firing Attachment) fitted to the muzzle; you sometimes see these yellow contraptions on the end of a weapon when watching TV dramas like Soldier Soldier or TV adverts about joining the Army.

During live firing or in real combat they would be using tracer rounds, which were usually loaded 1 in 4, so after every 3 rounds there would be a tracer round loaded, the tracer will glow at night and you can see the trajectory of the rounds and roughly where it is being fired.

The GPMG post called in a contact with the message "enemy down" there would be DI Staff (Directing Staff, used to direct and supervise exercises, different to the Drill Instructor) at the incident, monitoring the situation and giving advice as well as taking notes on certain actions, these would be fed back at the debrief at the end of the exercise, the DI Staff would usually be wearing an armband of some description to identify themselves. So, the DI Staff would tell the enemy that he was hit and whether he was wounded or KIA. If wounded they were given an A4 laminated sheet stating the injury, "gunshot to the leg or both arms blown off", this is so they can check if immediate first aid is being administered properly.

A medic and 2 others near the incident went forward to practice using their field dressing and simulating the administration of Morphine.

Next would be the Nuclear phase of the exercise. We would be briefed that enemy forces were stepping up their nuclear capability and may be using chemical weapons.

NBC Noddy suits would always be worn, and our respirators would always be carried. "GAS GAS GAS "and the loud banging of mess tins being banged together, both warnings of a chemical attack. NBC drills would be quickly carried out and the buddy-buddy checks are done exactly how this has been drilled into us since basic training.

Standing to in full NBC attire and all your kit with a weapon is not the nicest experience, but you do get used to it, as long as some twat of a DI doesn't use CS gas.

There was about 15 of 20 of us in this marquee at lunchtime just waiting for the next part of the exercise, others were out on guard or patrol. We were carrying our respirators, so it was a chance to grab some scran and shut eye. You never know when you are going to eat or sleep, so you grab a chance whenever you can, this is the reason that the military and veterans eat so fast, I am always finishing my meals before everyone else.

Suddenly there was a flash and bang at one end of the marquee, the place quickly filled with smoke, everyone was scrambling to get their respirators on whilst trying to get out.

A few of us including myself were overcome with smoke and were helped outside coughing and spluttering. We found out soon after that this was NOT part of the exercise and an enquiry was being started. It also asks questions about the training, a bit worrying if we had to mask in a real situation.

We then attended the farm building to visit the medic, a quick check-up and discharged. In the meantime, more contacts were taking place as you could hear the gunfire going on. We couldn't wait to get out there.

The farmhouse buildings were on a courtyard laced with grey cobblestones, at one end of the complex there was a large open arched gate a bit like a castle entrance, across the top was a walkway joining two of the building either side. on the right were the stables which we adapted for our HQ.

We went outside to join the firefight that was going on and had an immediate contact; 3 enemies were in the yard, one on the ground about 25 feet away searching one of our trailers parked in the open stables opposite and 2 others crossing the bridge connecting the outbuildings about 40 feet away. A warning was given by my oppo "Air Force Stop…. but before he could finish the sentence, "Air Force Stop or I will Fire!" the one on the ground turned and surrendered; he had no choice as his weapon was slung on his back and he didn't have time to retrieve it, cock it, aim it and then fire it; I don't think he thought that anyone was there. The other two on the bridge also stopped but turned towards us and as they raised their weapons; I was already in the aim position, SLR tight in my right shoulder, chin resting on the rear butt, the sling tight around my left wrist to help keep the weapon steady I aiming in the direction of the guy on the left whilst trailing my eye on the right guy. I opened fired. I let off 5 or 6 aimed shots in quick succession, switching aim back and forth, to ensure I hit them both. They both hit the deck. The DI confirmed 2 kills. The 2 "dead guys" both British Army were acting as enemy forces.

They came down from the bridge to debrief us. One of them played dead again, lying on his front. The others along with the DI went through body searching with us, looking to see if he was booby-trapped perhaps with a grenade under him. This was something that we were never taught as we were not expected to come across this sort of scenario in the Air Force.

Taceval and Minival

Taceval (tactical evaluation) and Minivals (mini evaluation) were thrown at us regularly, designed to test the speed in which a station can be manned. Minivals tended to be called in the early hours of the morning and last for the day, whereas a Taceval could last a few days and can be called at any time, and we usually would know that one would be called at some time as there would be behind the scenes planning going on and someone would inevitably tip a mate off and word would soon spread.

The call-out itself was the sound of the siren, the same ones used when there was about to be an air raid during the war. This sound can be heard for miles around and would surely have pissed off the locals, as dogs start barking and car alarms would be going off everywhere.

In July 1980, after a night at the NAAFI bop. Everyone was sound asleep; at about 0500hrs, the sirens started bellowing out its screams. A tannoy message would be read out by someone in the Station Guardroom "Exercise, Exercise, Exercise – all personnel are to report to their places of work immediately", this would have been repeated 2 or 3 times. Normally everyone would be jumping up, putting on their combats and while on the way out of the block, would be knocking on their neighbour's door to ensure he was up. Not this time, I don't know what it was? Was it a nice warm cosy dawn and everyone just wanted a few more minutes? or was it that everyone was still pissed from the night in the NAAFI?

The next thing I heard, was banging on my bedroom window and someone shouting at the top of his voice, "Get the f*ck up now you f*cking retards or you will all be charged" I was on the ground floor of Belvedere block which was the accommodation for Supply Sqn personnel only and had only recently been allocated this room. My room was facing one of the car parks, I imagine that I was one of the first he went for. I jumped up got changed, grabbed my "grab-bag" from under the bed and legged it down the corridor meeting, other lads, on the way. We ran across the car park, over the main road and up the loading ramp into R & D.

We all just fell about laughing as we may have just about have gotten away with that. We then found out that the guy shouting at the windows was, in fact, the Station Warrant Officer (SWO), he couldn't possibly know who had responded or who was still in bed.

A few days later, a newspaper article was printed in one of the red-top tabloids. The headline was "Flying Bedstead Squadron" it went on to state that "the sirens were sounded for a dawn call out at an RAF base, but the only place the airmen scrambled to, was further under their blankets" it continued that a "rocket" was given by the Station Commander stating, that he was going to fine everyone who didn't get up. Some names were taken, and 35 airmen were charged.

We were quite lucky in some respects being suppliers, or blanket stackers which other trades called us; it had its rewards. There are certain trades that everyone will want to befriend, cooks for extra rations, MT Drivers for free lifts to the pub, certain RAF Police who are sometimes good for a quick blue light taxi home after the bop and of course us suppliers! We were the ones with the newest kit, newest uniforms and shiny bits on the shelf in the storeroom. " You can't have that, someone might want it!" we were the pinnacle of all trades, piss us off and you would find out, maybe not immediately, it could be years down the line when you finally leave the RAF and you go to hand back your kit on your last day, and suddenly there is a list on your clothing book of stuff you have never seen in your life, you plead with the stacker but they just hand you a bill to pay for the missing kit, you can't get your blue departure card stamped until the bill is settled.

Every six months or so, you can get a chance to work in a different part of the Supply Squadron, I had just done stints in Tech Stores, P.O.L and Forward Supply, there were many other areas too which it would be possible to work in, like Clothing Stores or the Supply Accounts Flight. Because I had recently gained substantive driving experience and had already been on deployment, I was sent to MSF and I was to be part of 18 Squadron. If the squadron was to deploy on operations or exercise anywhere, I would go too as the squadron was part of the Quick Reaction Flight (QRF); others were attached to 33 Sqn Puma and 7 Sqn Chinook; if anything kicked off anywhere in the world and one of our squadrons were to be tasked by the MOD then we would be gone.

MSF was unique; you didn't learn anything about it in trade training as there were so few of them about. The building itself was on the edge of the airfield just passed the fire station. It was a single-story building with 2 large roller doors at each end so you could drive vehicles into to load up, it was a bit like a roll in roll out garage. Inside the building had offices and a crew room on one side and storage racks on the other. There was a distinct smell of canvas tarpaulins. All the shelves were filled with the stations' defence stores. Tents, kerosene heater, tilly lamps, shovels, water containers, empty jerry cans, field kitchens etc. Anything that may be required in a field on deployments. Everything was prepped and ready to go.

After a deployment of a squadron when the equipment was returned to us in MSF everything that had been opened were checked, any broken or missing items were replaced. We would then spread the canvas out on the grass outside, and "re-proof" it, we had to pour a proofing solution into a drip tray, the same as like they would put under a vehicle when doing an oil change, 2 or three of us would get our brooms and sweep the solution onto the canvas, making sure that it was completely covered. When dry we would turn them over and repeat. The tents would then be erected by us to ensure that 22 poles and spider connectors fitted snuggly. We became the fasted at erecting a 12 by 12 tent; even quicker than the RAF regiment who were the biggest users, we used to pair up and try and beat our quickest time from before, the times were recorded in the crew room notice board, just a bit of fun. Quite often individuals or groups may go for a weekend camping or night fishing and want to sign out equipment, and of course, we would expect something in exchange, a crate of beer was the usual currency! unless someone had something better to offer. Money was never used.

Not long after returning from a deployment somewhere it was not unusual to be told that you were going to go straight back out again! This was one of those occasions. We had just got back from a training exercise on Salisbury Plain with the Chinooks to be told we going to be Wales with a few of our "special friends" from Hereford and then over to West Germany for an unclassified training mission which involved a lot of low-level flying (hedge hoping) and the Special Forces (SF) guys would practice getting on and of the aircraft whilst we were still moving, over water and in and out on their dinghies. We got to know these guys quite well as we were always working with them in some capacity or another.

CHAPTER 4

My Falklands War

Three hundred miles from the most southern tip of Argentina sits the British claimed Falkland Islands. In 1982 an undeclared war between Argentina and the Britain started, it was to go on for 74 days.

The conflict began on 2 April, after Argentina invaded and occupied the islands. The following day the South Georgia was also invaded. The British government then put together and dispatched a naval task force to go to the South Atlantic to engage the Argentine Navy and Air Force before making the famous amphibious assault on the islands. The conflict lasted for 74 days and ended with Argentina surrendering on the 14 June, returning the back to British control.

On 2 April 1982, all training had been halted whilst an Op's briefing was taking place with all the officers, it was at this briefing that word had reached us that the Falkland Islands had been invaded by Argentina and that we were returning to the UK. We were stuck in Osnabruck West Germany on an exercise, having been there for about 3 weeks. The situation was being monitored back at Odiham via HQ Northwood, as tensions had been getting serious in South Georgia, where an Argentinian fishing boat had tried to overrun a small Royal Marines contingency stationed there.

The Commanding Officer (CO) came out of the briefing and called the rest of us together and gave the Endex.

Our new orders were to take down the camp and load the aircraft ready for departure back to the UK, with a precise time for take-off given. The aircrew disappeared into the ops tent; I presume to plan the return route, whilst all hands to deck, everyone pitched in to pack up.

The two land rovers were loaded into the back of two of the Chinooks and then backed up with all the tents, equipment and spares, the crewmen ensuring that everything was secure and tied down, a refuelling bowser full of aviation fuel pulled up and refuelled the Chinooks ready for take-off.

All the ground crew climbed into the back of one of the Chinooks, we were carrying our webbing and kit, but all our weapons were safely secured in their crates. There were only about 20 of us so we had quite a bit of room which made a change; it was to be a comfortable ride. The rotors started turning and winding up to take-off speed, the smell of aviation fuel was in the air, it reminded me of when we used to fly off on holiday when I was younger. Suddenly one of the techies on board noticed a small hydraulic leak in the roof of the aircraft under the rear rotor. He tapped the Air Loadmaster (Loadie) on the shoulder to get his attention and pointed to the leak, the Loadie quickly spoke to the pilot who immediately shut down the engines. Everyone de-bussed the aircraft and waited in the now empty field where only a few hours ago we had all our tents up. It seemed like an eternity before, the aircraft was given the thumbs up to take off and head home. The engines started up again and before we knew it, we were lifting and getting airborne.

We headed South-West towards Dortmund and then towards the Möhne Dam, that was a real treat; it was hard to believe that nearly 39 years ago, 617 Sqn flew here in their Lancaster's and bombed it with the "bouncing bombs". After this slight detour, we headed West towards the Dutch border, over the Netherlands and into Belgium, where we stopped at some military airfield for a refuel.

Then across the Channel over Dover and up to RAF Odiham.

On arrival, we quickly unloaded the Chinooks and unpacked the kit, returned our weapons to the armoury and then off for a well-deserved shower and a beer or 4!

The following morning, we reported to the squadron Op's room for a debrief. We were told we could stand down but had to leave our contact details with the Guardroom.

I returned home to London to visit my family and spent some quality time with Imelda. On one of the days, Mel and I jumped on a train and went to see some of her family who lived in another part of "The Smoke", we had only been there for a couple of few hours when the news came on. There was an announcement saying that "all military personnel on leave are to contact their units immediately".

I knew this was serious, like everyone else we had been, monitoring news bulletins on the TV watching for information on the events happening in the South Atlantic. We had to jump on a bus and then get the train from Victoria back down to Croydon. Victoria Station was eerie, there were serviceman everywhere, some in uniform, others in civilian clothes, all mingling together. There were notices written on chalked boards asking for military personnel to contact their units, the same message that was on the 6.00 o'clock news. We got to mum and dads to collect my car and my dad told me that someone from RAF Odiham had called and I was to return to camp; I grabbed my bag, said my goodbyes and left.

Imelda only lived 3 miles down the road in Carshalton, which was on the route so I thought it would be nice just to spend a little more time with her before I dropped her at her mum and dads. As we pulled up outside her house, Imelda's dad, Sean came out straight out to give me the same message about returning to camp.

Sean had served in the RAF during the war, he joined when he was just 15 years old, using his brother's passport as I.D as he wasn't old enough to join. After his basic training, he joined the RAF Police, I do not know if this was his choice or whether he was just seconded, he never spoke much about his time in the RAF but was proud to be involved with the guarding and escorting of Rudolf Hess when he was captured in Scotland. Mel's mum Bridie also served in the RAF in a general duties roll, she was in charge of ordering food for the catering squadron and also took some of the recruits on PT runs. One day on a cold wet morning she was walking back along Credenhill heading back to RAF Hereford when a Rolls Royce pulled up alongside and a Lady in the back wound down her window and offered Bridie a lift, I remember Bridie telling me this story with fondness. As she looked up and was about to accept the lift, she realised who it was. She quickly came to attention and threw up a salute "thank you but I cannot accept" she told her, "but thank you for the offer your Highness" to The Duchess of York, the future Queen.

On 4 April I returned to RAF Odiham Guardroom and was greeted by the Station Warrant Officer (SWO); he was an OK guy, strict when needed and compassionate when it was required, this time it was the latter. He checked my F1250 ID card put his hand on my shoulder and said, "good luck boy, be in the squadron hangar at 0900hrs in the morning for a briefing with the CO".

The briefing took place and lasted a few hours, we were told what we may expect and were given a list of personal kit to get ready, which at the time included new NBC suits and respirators! FFS, gas attack is all we need, now we were really worried, but soon after we were informed that the Argies didn't have the capability to launce Nuclear, Biological and Chemical attacks, so we could leave them behind. Luckily, being a Stacker had its perks. I was able to collect all new kit from my mates in Clothing Stores and also get some extra bits for my oppos on the Squadron.

The best bit of kit I kept for myself was a DPM windproof smock, which was good to provide an extra layer, (I still have it to this day). The only kit I didn't replace were my boots, these were broken in nicely.

It was a sombre moment as we now had to place our F1250s in an envelope we had to empty our wallets of photos of loved ones, bank cards and anything else that could give away our identities if we were unlucky to be captured and taken prisoner of war (POW) as interrogators have been known to use this information to try to get information from you, not that I knew much anyway.

We were issued with a copy of the Geneva Convention card. "Geneva prisoner of War Convention 1949" which was to be our new ID card, this had just my name, my name rank and number on it.

The card reads:

"This convention sets out the rules, internationally agreed, regarding the rights and treatment of prisoners of war during captivity.

It applies equally to our servicemen who are captured and to enemy servicemen who are taken prisoner by our forces.

Members of the regular Armed Forces are not the only persons entitled on capture to be treated as prisoners of war. Members of militia, volunteer corps, civilians holding military identity cards, seamen holding identity cards issued by the government and under certain conditions members of the resistance movements in occupied territories are also entitled to be so treated.In cases of doubt a captured person must be given the benefit of the doubt and treated initially as a prisoner of war.

All prisoners are entitled to humane and respectful treatment and must be protected from Acts of violence, intimidation, insults, and public curiosity, reprisals against them are forbidden".

The hardest part was that we had to write personal letters home, these were handed into the Sqn Adjutant and would be given one to Mel and one to my mum and dad in the event of my death. Then I wrote my will! On leaving the briefing we were issued with 3 SLR magazines and a cleaning kit – we were now ready to go!

"Stay safe. Be vigilant and check your 6s" was written on the crew-room wall. Military talk for mind your back!

25 April 1982, having been on standby for the best part of 3 weeks, we were put on 4 hours standby; the SS Atlantic Conveyor was loaded and had set sail from Southampton towards the Ascension Islands.
During the standby period, we were confined to barracks, unless we were on specific off-site duties relating to the deployment. We had to make lots of trips up and down the A3 to Southampton to deliver all of our equipment from weapons, tents, rations, field kitchens, Houchin generators and helicopter spares which were carefully packed away in "Fly Away Packs" for the Chinooks we were deploying with, the list was endless.

Other personnel on duty were tasked with getting the kit ready back at RAF Odiham and re-loading the vehicles as they came back. There was even a Puma helicopter from 33 Sqn involved in the moves. In Southampton, we had crews who were working around the clock recording and loading shipping containers which when full, were lifted onto the back of the SS Atlantic Conveyor.

This was part of the largest logistical operation ever carried out in the UK and in the quickest possible time. Ships were being converted to carry troops, and aircraft and even make-shift helicopter pads were erected on what were normally cruise liners. Thousands of personnel from all 3 services and the merchant navy were working together. In all 127 ships were made ready to move.

News reached us that the British nuclear submarine, HMS Conqueror, had been tracking the Argentine ship the General Belgrano. She posed a threat so and under the 'Rules Of Engagement', fired 3 torpedo's sinking her.

3rd May, we were told to make our way to the armoury to collect our weapons. As we waited for the armoury hatch to open, everyone was talking about yesterday's sinking of the General Belgrano. Morale was high, we had sunk one of theirs; then we get hit with a 'bombshell'; news filters through that HMS Sheffield was hit by 2 Exocet missiles, killing 20 and injuring another 26. The mood changed. Everyone was now quiet, I moved slowly to the hatch and was passed my weapon, I checked if it was clear, (no rounds in it), I cleared the working parts forward, fired off the action and applied my safety catch as drilled many times.

Everyone else did the same, Sterling Sub Machine Guns (SMGs) for the Officers and SNCOs, the aircrew had 9mm browning pistols and the rest of us collected our SLRs. The RAF Regiment (Rock Apes) carried their array of weapons plus the GPMGs which were to be mounted 2 into each of the Chinooks, one at the rear and one on the side starboard forward door. This had now become real! We were now awaiting our window to move, which was to be on 5 May.

I was one of 2 suppliers amongst the technicians, aircrew, RAF Regiment and medics who were on the coach which were to take us to RAF Lyneham for onwards transition to the Ascensions.

We stayed at Lyneham overnight, before we boarded an RAF VC10 which was to take us to the Ascension Islands via Dakar. We landed on Ascension Island on the 6th May with nothing to do except wait whilst we were watching different units from all services depart on helicopters out to their respective ships. I managed to get a quick helicopter flight on a Sea King over to the SS Atlantic Conveyor to drop off 15 of our techies who were sailing on her. Their task was to get the Chinooks ready when they got closer to the war zone. I spent a few hours just checking our equipment and also loaded some beer and crisps "just in case we needed it sometime". Then I bagged a lift back to the shore on a Gazelle.

On the 7th May the MV Norland had just arrived to join the Amphibious Task Group. It was now our turn, we were given the green light to go; I collected my kit and climbed aboard one of our Chinooks which was staying on the Island and were flown over to the Norland, which was anchored amongst a Task Force of ships about a quarter of a mile out to sea.

The Norland was a roll on roll off passenger ship that went into service in 1971 but was requisitioned by the M.O.D to be used to ferry troops to the Falklands. We landed on a makeshift helipad at the aft end of the ship. We were then given the order to move and in 2 files we were led out of the rear of the aircraft, rotors still turning, you had to be careful of the downdraft; it had been known to blow guys over, and I didn't fancy being blown overboard. We were marshalled by one of our squadron guys who had sailed from the UK on her, he was to assign accommodation and show us the way to our cabins below on C deck.

The corridors and stairways were narrow, but the floors were completely scuffed and had boot polish from all the troops already on board. It was difficult trying to move whilst carrying all this equipment and a weapon, and then you face a barrage of abuse from members of 2 Para taking the piss. The Paras were a good bunch of guys, very professional and hard as f*ck! we were lucky as we knew some of them from previous exercises, and they were only based a few miles down the road from us in Aldershot army garrison.

I grabbed my pit space on the bottom bunk, as it had a small bedside table next to it and settled down for the "cruise".

Three Stripes, I'm Out

On the 8th May the War Cabinet back in the UK, gives the message "to dispatch the landing force from Ascension Islands – God Save The Queen"!

CHAPTER 5

Britannia Rules The Waves

The sea is calm, the sun is hot, ships funnels all around churning out smoke as the Task Force sets sail from Ascension Island. The ships tannoy is playing Rule Britannia and everyone is out on the decks, not believing that this was happening. What was going through everyone's minds, was everyone at home ok?

Some helicopters were still flying stores from the jetty onto various ships, as we move further away, this stopped, the only sounds now were ships engines and the chat amongst ourselves.

For the next 2 weeks, this will be our home. Plenty was going on around the ship. Contingents from the Paras were on circuit training on the flight deck, a volleyball court was erected on another deck, good job they had plenty of balls, I'd seen at least 3 land in the sea during the first day. The competition was good, as one of the PTI's arranged an interservice competition, which was eventually won by a mixed team of unattached servicemen. We were all encouraged to join in with various activities, I did have a go at the volleyball, it was never my game. But the 3-a-side footy below decks was good a good laugh, though very hot; it was great for weight loss.

The food onboard was first class, a real credit to the ship's company, even to our own cooks who went and did some culinary delights with them. We were allowed to drink on board but there was a maximum of 3 cans per troop. To help restrict the amount of alcohol each person had, you had to purchase "beer-chits", little green slips of paper the size of a postage stamp, you'd hand one to the barman, he would give you a small can of beer. In the evening we would be entertained by the ships' company or sometimes a serviceman might pick a guitar and play something from Floyd or Genesis. Wendy (as he liked to be called), the ships resident performer, was a fine pianist who would play anything that was requested. Normally he would play the keys quietly in the background whilst the Paras gambled away on the card table.

At one of these card schools, with over 100 of us watching this game of poker, two paras were head to head; there must have been over £300 all in loose change, when eventually the game ended, the winner had collected all this change, every pocket was bulging and his beret was full of all this change. God only knew what he was going to do with it, there was only a small shop onboard that opened twice a day selling chocolate, cigarettes and soft drinks.

A few days later, we approached the Equator and in a good-old military fashion we got ready to celebrate. All the ships company gathered up on the decks to witness the event; some RN and RMs dressed up as pirates in readiness for when the ship crossed the Equator. In the Navy, this is known as the "crossing the line ceremony where we (the ships company) will be presented to Neptune's Court to pay tribute to the Lord of the Seas. Two men were singled out from the audience, it turns out that these were the 2 youngest on board. As part of the court proceedings, fictional charges were read out and they were both made to drink a large alcoholic beverage. To end the event, we were all given a tot of rum to celebrate as we crossed the Equator. This was the first time that I had tasted rum and it wasn't the last, it is my favourite tipple, even to this day. A ships briefing was to follow now by a senior officer on board, we were told now, that all entertainment will stop, and the bar will no longer be open. We were now a target and must be ready for any eventuality that came our way.

Fitness training was scaled down, so there would be minimum movement on the ship, this was so you knew roughly where your squadron, platoon, regiment was located onboard.

Live firing was scheduled for the 11th and 12th and at the crack of dawn it started. From the rear of the ship, you could hear the sound of GPMGs, rattling away, then followed the sound of SLRs being fired rapidly. The targets were all the gash bags from the ship's galley, they were being thrown in and we used the weapons to destroy them we saw this as a chance to zero our weapons whilst feeding the fish.

13th May. From now on there would be silence on board, then "Action Stations, Action Stations" is announced over the ships tannoy. Our instructions were to stay in our cabins, however, if we were already on deck and time didn't permit us to return to our cabin, then we would man a weapon; the rumour going around was that there was a strong possibility that we were being tracked by a submarine.

"Stand-down, Stand-down, all available hands are to report to the decks immediately" was the next message, wondering what the f*ck this was all about, the 4 of us grabbed our weapons and helmets and joined everyone else in the corridor trying to get up the narrow stairs. On arrival outside in the sunshine, we were greeted with the most spectacular sight seen yet. What they thought was a submarine was actually, a large school of whales on the surface. The ship's radar had picked up a large mass travelling towards the fleet.

The task force continued on its voyage, we were not getting much information back from what was happening elsewhere and we still did not know at this time what the landing plans were, though we knew that our C.O had had a brief from No. 10, the information was classified and on a need to know basis only.

14 May. The threat level has just been increased to Critical, the highest level available; indicating an attack could be imminent. Active service has now been declared. All the ships company have assembled in the main restaurant, those in first managed to get the comfy settees, then the tables and chairs, the rest of us standing at the back. We are given the news that 3 Argentine Skyhawks had been engaged and destroyed yesterday but HMS Glasgow had sustained damage during the contact. We were informed that 5 Infantry Brigade were on their way down on the QE2.

From now on, there would be no smoking on the outer decks, all windows were to be kept blacked out and movement onboard was to be kept to a minimum.
Non-essential personnel would be used as guards, that included us, as we were pretty much redundant now,

anyway it would give us something to do. The Para's would be tasked with their duties as they were mostly below decks from now on prepping. Guns would be placed all around the decks and would be manned 24/7 either GPMGs or SLRs, we didn't have the luxury of the big guns as used on the battleships around us. We were in the "Total Excursion Zone".

"RED RED RED" this tannoy message we would hear daily, sometimes 3 or 4 times within a few hours.
The bridge officers would receive regular messages from our escort ships if they picked-up anything on their radar.

We would then be given the "all clear".

We were well drilled in the abandon ship, if we came under attack and the ship got damaged, we would don our lifejackets and help fight fires or whatever needed doing at that time, we would be guided by a senior naval rating or the ships own crew.

19 May at about 06.00hrs we were woken by the daily tannoy announcement, but this wasn't the usual "Good morning shipmates, today's weather is wet; the duty-free shop will open at 0900hrs", no, we got:
"Rule Britannia!
Britannia rules the waves
Britons never, never, never shall be slaves."
"There will be an O Group with all hands at 09.00hrs"

We all assembled in our usual fashion; first in gets the settee and boy did we move but still managed to end up standing at the back.

The mood had changed there was no larking about or banter, we were given the news that 2 Para will be the first to land on the Islands. We were going in. This is what we had all been waiting for, this is what we trained for. The only thing that we didn't know was where and when as that was on a strictly need to know basis.
We now just had to wait!

21/22 May D-Day, along with HMS Broadsword who was giving us cover with Sea Wolf surface to air missiles. We did a recce around Fanning Head which is at the entrance into the Falkland Sound, or Bomb Alley as it was known, then we sailed slowly into the sound with HMS Broadsword just behind us, we were the first ship in. I found out years later that we were sent in on the Norland as bait; there had been intelligence from the SAS that Fanning Head had been mined. In Sandy Woodward's book – 100 Days, he admitted sending in a ship to see if it was clear.

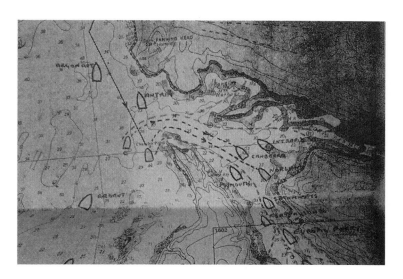

It was raining, the cloud was low, and the visibility was poor. Perfect for Operation Sutton to start, the name given to the landings by 2 Para. It was in the early hours, the lights were off whilst a Landing Craft Utility boat (LCU) from HMS Fearless piloted by the Royal Marines came alongside, the ship's doors were already open and 2 Para started to make their way on to the LCU. I could not recognise any of them as they all looked the same, all camouflaged in their combats and wearing life jackets, which I expected they would discard on the LCU when they reached the shore in a few minutes. As each LCU pulled away, the next would pull up, load and leave. After the last one pulled away heading to Blue Beach, we closed the doors and waited.

Daylight soon approached and I get my first call to go on Bridge Watch, 4 hours on 2 hours off, on stag. I was located on the port side of the ship outside the Bridge wing, my only shield was a glass panel in front, which acted as a windbreak for the bridge and on my left were some railings with a GPMG mounted on and I was carrying my weapon. Inside the Bridge I could see the Captain, the Ships first Officer and the COs of some of the military groups still on board; Wg Cdr Tony Staples was our representative and I could see another of one our guys on the Starboard door. The CO glanced in my direction and gave an acknowledging nod and then turned his head and did the same to my oppo on the other side. It was a bit of a morale booster to know that the CO was with us on this.

The CO did not see it necessary for us to be issued with ammunition at this time the only ones who were fully armed were the Rocks on the GPMGs. The Aircrew and SNCOs who were all carrying loaded submachine guns, which would be useless in this type of combat. Then there was me, I had a GPMG next to me which I had only ever fired once in my life on an exercise. I'm carrying my SLR with 3 empty mags, I've got no protection from "incoming" and a bloody Matelot was standing next to me with his SLR made ready. He did nothing but keep saying "how the f*ck am I supposed to shoot a jet down with an SLR", "likewise buddy," I said, "I'd have to throw mine at it".

We were anchored somewhere at the furthest point in Bomb Alley facing the way that we came in. My lookout point was over "Wreckpoint" which was a mountain, just past Ajax Bay at Bomb Alleys entrance on the left, this was given the name "Point Charlie". Point Alfa was to my rear (port side); Bravo to my immediate left, I could also see Delta on the opposite side to the Sound.

Everyone else had their own lookout points which overlapped to ensure that a complete 360degree Arc of Fire was covered, giving us all-round protection.

The first wave of Argentine aircraft was airborne and heading our way. We just 'wait out' now!

Suddenly, over the horizon I spot an aircraft dropping out of the clouds over Point Charlie, I clicked on my radio, "Aircraft over Point Charlie, Captain", I knew that everyone had already seen it, as I heard the sound of Lenny and Canada cocking their the GPMGs on the bridge roof getting them ready for some AA. We waited for the AC to come closer, it was a Mk3 Skyhawk, then all hell broke loose, there was gunfire from the GPMGs above me, the Matelot emptied his magazine of 20 rounds in rapid-fire, then he switched to the GPMG, I buddied up with him to help feed the belt of ammunition whilst he fired, guns were going off from all directions, the smell of cordite in the air, then "woosh, woosh" as 2 Sea Wolf missiles were fired off in succession from one of the ships nearby, the Skyhawk fired off a couple of bursts, then banked away quickly from us back towards Charlie. As he dipped over a mountain a Sea Wolf that was fired from a ship caught up with him just as he was going behind a mountain and out of sight, we saw smoke appear, we assumed it was hit. I was completely helpless and well pissed off at not being able to fire, but it was an experience of indirect death that I was to witness from behind my glass shield. Then the second wave, then the third and so forth, attack after attack. The Argentine Air Force were at it big time.

During some downtime in the attacks, I was back in my cabin. The adrenaline was still rushing through me, but as I relaxed, I started to shake, this was a point in my life that I never thought I would experience. I couldn't stop thinking about that first attack, my first sight of the enemy; I started to ask myself questions, who was the pilot? Did he bale out? All sorts of thoughts were going through my head.

Shortly after there was a knock on the door and in walked one of the Crewmen, FS Gutherie, he was one of the decent loadmasters, a real gent. There was no waiting to be invited in, you just knock and go! He asked if I was OK and then told me that I was supposed to be manning the cargo deck with him and should have been there half an hour ago at 0300 hrs., "I just said "f*ck, sorry, I came off shift and must have fallen asleep". He warned me that if it was one of the other crewmen I may well have been put on a charge and then court-martialled. However, after all, I was the person that everyone wanted to know and I had the key to the treasure chest, the main store's container on the Atlantic Conveyor with all the goodies in.

Standing Orders had now been changed, we were going to be fully armed, the CO was aware of what happened after that first attack as he was on the bridge and was concerned for everyone's safety, I am not sure if that was a good thing or not, arming airmen with live ammunition! We got issued with an initial 60 rounds each. I loaded 20 into each of my magazines 1:4 tracer rounds, I clipped one onto my SLR and placed the other two into my ammo pouch.

I was making my way to the bridge for another stag when I heard "RED RED RED" over the tannoy I had to move quickly as I didn't want to be exposed with no cover from incoming. Just as I got there a Sky Hawk was banking low

in the Sound firing at the "Big White Whale", the SS Canberra which was anchored about 50 metres from us, it fired, missed and turned away and then started to climb, it was closely followed by a Sea Harrier making chase. As watched in anticipation the Sea Harrier let fire a sidewinder and scored a direct hit.

24 May Our time on the Norland was to come to an end; we were being moved to get ready to support the rest of the squadron when it arrived on the Atlantic Conveyor. We were told we would be joining the assault ship, HMS Fearless just across the water, but that would be picked up from Fox Bay. We were about to get ready to move when there was another air raid. This time the attack was on us, but they missed with two 500lb bombs; they dropped either side of the ship.

We boarded a Wessex helicopter on the helipad. Its rotors were still turning, so it would get a quick take off, that way we are not exposed for too long, especially as we had just been attacked. The Wessex did not waste any time, we didn't even fasten our seatbelts, we were up flying at a low level and before we knew it, we had landed on the water's edge at Fox Bay. We climbed up the muddy bank onto a grass area, only to be met by 2 hairy Special Forces (SF) guys carrying M16 assault rifles, "what the f*ck are you lot doing here" one said, the other guy pointed at some overgrown grass area and bluntly said "take cover there and stay the f*ck out of our way". I think they were a bit pissed off as they thought the Wessex was a resupply flight with rations and ammo, but no, they got 30 crabs!

We set up an all-round defence position and waited for the next move. There was one air raid, but no shots were fired to or from our little area.

Soon an LCU came alongside, turned then reversed onto the beach area lowering the ramp; we approached it with some caution as none of us had ever had any training in amphibious warfare and didn't want to end up in the water.

We all got on safely and the LCU moved away in the direction of HMS Fearless which we could see ahead of us.

We docked into the back of HMS Fearless I was immediately issued with our anti-flash gear and lifejacket, which we would carry with us all the time.

We were shown down to our mess or cabin as the Navy call it. The beds were 3 high bunks with a stack on each side with a small gap for one person at a time to climb in or out of. In our cabin was one of our gunners, four matelots and me. The cabin was also used by four other matelots, so they had to double bunk with each other, but not at the same. Luckily, we were just there for cover and would not be undertaking any duties, but we were expected to respond to all emergency drills.

Each time we went in or out of the cabin we would have to close the water hatch behind us, this was in case the ship took on water, we would be contained until help arrived if it did at all. We were to stay on board until the carrier force with Atlantic Conveyor came alongside; the plan was to join some of the other squadron guys who sailed down on her from Southampton all those weeks ago. We would go on board to sort out the logistics to get the Chinooks and all our stores off.

Air attack followed; air attack, we (the fleet) were bombarded. The following morning, I was awoken by a very loud bang, a bit like someone hitting the sides of the ship with a big sledgehammer, I grabbed my anti-flash gear and donned my helmet and waited. One of our matelots told us that the bang we heard was a depth charger being dropped in case there were any submarines about.

Further air attacks continued. It was a difficult time being stuck in a steel box, not knowing much of what was going on outside. We were getting some commentary, but not a lot. We then heard that we had taken 3 casualties from shrapnel after a bombing run and that we picked up a downed Argentine pilot; he would be treated for any injuries then interrogated, but hopefully not like in the movies.

25 May, we were just queuing to get some scran (Navy slang for food) when our FS came to us in little groups to give us the most horrendous news. The Atlantic Conveyor had been hit with 2 Exocet missiles; the mood was gone it was very sad, our heads dropped in disbelief, "Are our guys ok" I remember asking, to which the reply was "Dazz, I don't know!" "We are waiting for further news".

A few hours later we were called together to be told that we had lost 3 of the 4 Chinooks, the Atlantic Conveyor was burning but all our guys were picked up by a lifeboat. The Atlantic Conveyor was still afloat

There were 22 lives lost on her, including the Captain who refused to leave the ship.

Everything thing we had, 3 Chinooks, aircraft spares, tents, ammo, rations, porn mags, beer and crisps, they were all lost to the sea, lost forever! The hierarchy had to decide what to do with us. We only had one Chinook, Bravo November, (BN) which was airborne when the Conveyor was hit, but we had no spares to keep her flying and no landing base for her.

Twenty-seven of our guys stayed ashore during this part of the conflict to support Bravo November at Port San Carlos settlement.

Port San Carlos was on the north side of bomb alley on the west side of East Falklands.

The locals called it KC, which was named after a former owner called Keith Cameron. San Carlos itself was named after the ship which once visited in the 1700s.

As soon as we heard about the Atlantic Conveyor, Dave Vivian, my corporal, asked to go onboard before she finally sunk to try and get off as much of the FAP. Unfortunately as they were trying to arrange this she sank. The rest of us were cross-decked to another ship whilst we waited for the MV Europic Ferry to arrive with more chinooks on board and spares, but that was about a week away still. Dave and the team lived in a garage at first but then went to luxury accommodation in the sheep pens where they got it all ready for when we joined them ashore. Dave went over the island in a helicopter to try and scrounge as much food and anything else he could get his hands on.

On one sortie Bravo November had to make a quick descent after losing visibility in a sudden snow shower; she hit the water damaging the fuselage and its antennas, if that wasn't enough, the co-pilot decided to eject his door. The pilot, Sqn Ldr Langworthy managed to pull up with the rotors rattling away and water pouring back out of the cabin through a hole in the floor, now he had the problem of retuning to base; they were freezing cold, wet and unable to communicate with us.   On approach he turned on all of the lights in the cabin as well as the landing lights, it completely lit up the sky; the pilot assumed that we would know it was not an enemy aircraft and this was the only way he could land it without us shooting it down; it was successful, he landed. We had all taken up firing positions before someone realised it was our Bravo November. If we had shot it down, half of us and the locals in the settlement we were protecting may have perished and the war would have been lost because Bravo November was the only aircraft that had such a vast carrying capability and it was essential for the war effort.

During the conflict we moved over 1500 troops, 95 wounded or dead, 650 POW and over 550 tons of equipment.

We now had a Chinook with no communications and no left-hand door. We did, however, manage to grab a door off the Argentinian chinook which was shot down on the outskirts of Stanley Racecourse, we also managed to recover many other spares that we could use, including a service manual that was written in Spanish!

6 June. My sergeant, Dave Hougham along with 4 Chinooks and more spares had finally arrived on the MV Contender Bezant. I was flown over on a Gazelle and was dropped off onto a makeshift helipad. I was greeted by Dave and taken to the mess for a cuppa and catch up, it was good to see him. Dave had been in the RAF since

1967 when he joined as an apprentice, back in those days, there was an apprentice scheme, nowadays, it was straight in do your training and then you were qualified! Dave was a blonde lad who came from Guildford, Surrey he was born in an ex-WW2 Nissan hut which was used to house families up until about the early '50s. Quite fitting that he was destined to join the military.

He had been in charge of clothing stores when I left for the Falklands, I had no idea he was on his way. He was given his orders to move 2 weeks before we lost the Atlantic Conveyor. When she was hit on the 25 May, Dave and his team spent the next 3 days and nights getting spares ready, they even stripped 3 chinooks that were being serviced of any part that we could use. On his way down he was tirelessly putting the FAPs together. Like us on the Norland, it was weapon training and fitness with the Paras.

We sorted out some spares that I needed, and we strapped together 2 stacked rotor blades in their STCs.

The chinook blades are 30 feet long and fit nicely into its box which is about 2 ft longer than the blade, the boxes look like long metal coffins. Dave marshalled one of the chinooks going ashore onto the aft end of the ship, we loaded the spares on, and I strapped myself into my seat next to the Rock manning his GPMG on the crew door on the starboard side. The aircraft lifted slowly into a hover just above the deck, the loadie opened the centre hook door and lowered down the cargo hook. The chinook is fitted with a triple hook system which provides stability when carrying extra-large loads like armoured vehicles. It can also carry multiple loads to several destinations, a real workhorse. Dave and a technician hooked the blades up and signalled to the loadie who was hanging out the cargo door, the all-clear for take-off. The Loadmaster then relayed to the pilot to go and he closed the doors. The chinook's nose dipped slightly, and we lifted into the air, changing direction at the same time. I could see a couple of ships dotted around, as we headed towards the shoreline, I did wonder what they were doing; probably watching us wondering the same thing. Now over land, I was a bit more relaxed, I didn't know our location, but knew we could receive anti-aircraft fire. I just wasn't keen on being shot down over the water and having to swim.

We were flying at about 250ft heading towards our base at Port San Carlos; we picked up speed to avoid any anti-air attack, we were swinging left to right in a snake-like motion, the next thing we hear is "bang" and the floor opened up just in front of where I was sitting, a hole appeared. The aircraft then steadily swooped around and banked to one side, you could hear the sound of the rotors straining as we slowed and turned in a circular motion, as the pilot was changing direction, the gunner told me that we dropped the blades and they landed smack bang in the middle of an Argie minefield, it landed upright in the peat, below, someone at the front shouted

"180" everyone on board just burst out laughing, you wouldn't think that just a few moments earlier we could have all died.

At the enquiry it was said that the blade box swung like a pendulum as we hit a crosswind, the load became unstable and dangerous, so it had to be jettisoned. A few hundred thousand pounds worth of rotors: as if we didn't already enough problems with spares. Nothing more was said!

All the junior ranks were living in sheep sheds at the top of the jetty; it was a steep climb up a mud bank to get there, the path was just wide enough to reverse a LWB Land Rover up and was about 50 metres long. When you go down to the end the jetty bears to the left and the road to the right; I say road, it was a mud trail which led into a very large peat area, which was the size of a football pitch. On the far side was the settlement which housed some of the locals, at the far end was our office, which was a couple of ships ISO containers and two 12 by 12 tents. Just next to us was the makeshift aircraft pan where the Chinooks sat.

Behind us was John and Mandy's house, more about them later.

The aircrew and SNCOs stayed in one of the resident's houses. There were 35 locals in all scattered around the settlement and we got to know them all. Our accommodation was nothing like I had ever experienced in my life. A sheep shed! In the sheep sheds there were animal pens around built with wooden planks partitioning them, the same as a horse stable and no bigger than 8ft x4ft; just enough room to put a camp bed in, a small camping stool and a kerosene heater plus my kit. My weapon was always with me; at night it would snuggle up in my sleeping bag, extremely uncomfortable, but providing me with some comfort that if we were attacked, I knew exactly where it was. The plan would be to unzip my maggot, rollout, grab a magazine of 20, which was under my makeshift pillow, load, cock the weapon and fire. All good in my mind, never going to happen if the going gets tough!

We wrapped our groundsheets over the sides of our individual pens to try and get some privacy. At the end was the trough where they sheared the sheep and slaughtered them by cutting their throats, a quick death.

Our state-of-the-art shower system was knocked up by one of the ground techies, a 45-gallon oil drum with some pipes welded to it, the lit coal drives the hot water up the pipe and out of a hole and gives a nice shower flow, the only thing is it cannot be operated on its own, a buddy needs to slowly pour cold water into the drum using a water jerry can.

One weekend after the surrender, some of the locals came up to shear the sheep, and asked who wanted a go, well I and a few others were up for that, I was given some clippers after being showed how to hold the sheep. I got down on one knee placed my left arm around it, turned on the clipper and went for the wool, and crash, the bastard kicked out and I went flying.

Mail from home was something we all looked forward to receiving, somehow it would come down on a replenishment run, the Royal Mail would deliver to the Forces Sorting Office at Mount Pleasant near Mill Hill in London. They would sort it into units, squadron, ships. Bag and deploy. These mail bags would then be transferred down to Brize Norton or Lyneham to be flown by VC10 into Ascension, then loaded onto a ship or

Hercules which deliver to the islands for distribution to the troops. Letters to and from home were free to send, but you had to use a special blue airmail letter known as a bluey. But because the postman doesn't deliver to our doors at the same time every day, we would get 5, 6 or even 10 at a time. So, everyone used to number them in the top left corner of the envelope, so we knew which order to read them. On one mail delivery, I received a couple of parcels sent from home. Dad, Imelda and my old colleagues from AGI put together a parcel for me which contained, cigarettes, chocolate, sweets a cake and a roll of soft toilet paper. There was an article in one of the tabloids that us troops were complaining about the sheets of tracing paper in the ration packs, the funny thing about it was, that I wasn't the only one to get one. My other parcel came from Michele or Mitch as she liked to be called, Mitch is my cousin and we were very close and still are; she was the sister that I never had, indeed we call each other Bro and Sis. Along with more chocolate and sweets, she sent me a Crystal Palace scarf; this scarf went on every detachment after that and now hangs proudly in my son's bedroom.

The Sun newspaper used to send things out of the troops, but the Daily Mirror had the best one. Crates and crates were loaded onto a Hercules with bottles of "Task Force Ale".

The RAF expedited this on one trip, I do not think the RAF had anything else on board, except for the beer. I believe we were one of the first squadrons to get ours, I still have mine, albeit, empty.

The Chinooks continued doing their sorties, as our troops advanced on to their objective, we were starting to get some information on what was happening from our aircrew whenever they returned as we were allowed to go to the debriefs. 14 June, a normal day for us at Port San Carlos, but this was about to change, and history would be written. Sqn Ldr Langworthy was on a sortie near Stanley when news broke about a surrender. He immediately radioed to us "The white flag is flying over Stanley"

*This surrender is to be effective from **2359** hours ZULU on **14** June (**2059** hours local) and includes those Argentine Forces presently deployed in and around Port*

*Stanley, those others on East Falkland, (**Menendez's** **signature**) West Falkland and all outlying islands.*
*[**Menéndez's signature**] Commander Argentine Forces*
*[**Moore's signature**] J. J. MOORE Major General*
*[**Pennicott's signature**] Witness*
***2359** hours **14 June** 1982*

In a telex message to the Commander-in-Chief Fleet General Moore reports: *"In Port Stanley at 9 pm Falkland Island time tonight, 14th June 1982, Major General Menéndez surrendered to me all the Argentine Armed Forces in East and West Falkland, together with their impedimenta. Arrangements are in hand to assemble the men for return to Argentina, to gather in their arms and equipment, and to mark and make safe their ammunition.*

"The Falkland Islands are once more under the Government desired by their inhabitants. God Save the Queen."

CHAPTER 6

Coming Home

After the surrender it would still be another four weeks before we left for home; we were one of the last squadrons to leave. Operational sorties were continuing, POWs were being gathered up, medical attention was given and clothing and food before boarding the Norland to be repatriated back to Argentina.

Our wounded and the dead were the first to be sent home, although many were buried in graves near to where they fell, which were dug by their own troops. Some were buried at sea. These are now sacred memorials to them.

I got a chance to go to Port Stanley by Wessex helicopter to pick up some rations that had been flown in; I was with one of the rocks. We took off and headed over to Stanley, the flight was only about 15 minutes, then we got the nod to get ready to get off as the pilot had to head off somewhere else, we grabbed our webbing and made ready our weapons. The helicopter touched down and we got out of the side door, and onto a firm but peaty landing area, which was part of the paddock on the racecourse; the helicopter lifted off and we were ushered away to a portacabin on the side of the racecourse we had our IDs checked and then we climbed into the back of a Land Rover and whisked across into the capital.

The racecourse was alongside the harbour behind some houses. The houses were all bricks and mortar, but some had been painted different colours, it looked like something out of a children's tv program. One had a hole in its roof, where a rocket had hit it, I believe that one of the civilians that were killed, was in the house.

It was like being in a time warp, all the houses were weathered, the roads were a bit like ours and they drove on the left, but the Argies during their short occupancy insisted everyone drove on the right.

There is an old wreck beached in Whalebone Cove, at the end of Stanley harbour, which is overlooked by Mount Tumbledown, which just a few nights ago, witnessed some of the most fierce close quarter combat ever seen in recent times by British Forces.

We were dropped at our RV point and sent towards a pile of pallets up on a bank. The only way we could get to it was by walking along the road by some civilian houses and up the other side; a Chinook would pick us up later.

As we were walking, POWs were being taken towards a jetty, where some ships were going to take them back home, we could see the Norland anchored out in the harbour, with another ship.

The locals were glad to get rid of them, they were dirty bastards, when they occupied the locals' houses, they didn't use the toilets, no, they shat anywhere, they put faeces in fuse boxes for some reason, they filled one car glove box with it, on the bedroom floor, it was just everywhere.

We carried on with our stroll minding our own business when we noticed some British army officers and SNCOs were walking towards us, we braced up to pay our compliments as we were not wearing berets, so couldn't salute, one officer saluted back, when all of a sudden there was this bellowing at us, "why the f*ck have you got your magazines on your weapons, - you do know they have surrendered, remove them now you f*cking retards". Well, there's us shitting ourselves, we removed the magazines as ordered, and followed the safety action drill that had been drummed into us, then we did the first cock of the weapons simultaneously, we both ejected a live round onto the floor. At this point he was screaming at us wanting to know who we were as we didn't have any insignia showing. "RAF 18 Sqn," I said. "I might have f*cking known it had to be the f*cking crabs". Get the f*ck out of here you cunts".

We spent the rest of the afternoon, sitting around eating compo, whilst making sure the pongos didn't nick the duty frees, the Chinook turned up and the loadie got off to help us load the booze.

By now we had established our Forward Supply Flight, it was a great little setup, our office was in an ISO container, we had a bar set up in a tent, just on the other side, the Rocks had also set up a bar and named it the

"Goose and Brick" there were rumours as to how the name was given, the feathers gave it away, but at the time nothing was admitted.

There was a house just up at the top of our site, where John and Mandy McLeod lived, they were there during the invasion and stayed put! They lived on the islands for several years and a had a daughter called Lou, who was about 2 years old. We spent many evenings with them, Mandy used to make the most delicious Upland Goose pies for us. Whilst the pie was cooking in their peat Aga, Mandy would be cutting everyone's hair, we had a few sessions downing a few beers with John.

The day finally arrived; our replacements flew in the day before, we were not spending too much time handing over, as they knew exactly what to do, we just needed to show them where everything was, get our kit packed and move out the sheep shed, so they could move in.

We flew by Chinook to Port Stanley airport, which was renamed RAF Port Stanley. The Hercules aircraft was waiting on the pan we climbed aboard with all our kit, cramped up like sardines; rows and rows of military guys all heading home.

All our kit was stowed under our legs the person sitting opposite had his legs intertwined with mine this was done from one part of the aircraft to the other we looked like a giant zip, we had to endure this for 15 hours. Going

112

to the toilet in a funnel behind a curtain you had to climb over everything and everyone just to get your willy out into the tube and piss. Having a dump? Forget it, that was not going to happen.

We eventually arrived at Ascension Islands to be met an RAF VC10 to take us straight on to Brize Norton in Oxfordshire. I don't remember much of the journey, from the Falklands to Ascension Island, I must have slept for most of if it.

We were briefed, our equipment and our luggage was transferred and before we knew it, we were climbing the aircraft steps to take us home to Blighty.

We had our papers checked and handed in our ammunition, which was to stay on the islands, but my weapon was my responsibility and stayed with me. This was my first flight on a VC10 and the first time I was flying backwards, the seats on a VC10 all face to the rear, I didn't like travelling on a train like that, so I definitely wasn't going to like this or so I thought! No sooner than we took off, I fell asleep.

The flight time was about 8 hours, I woke only to eat and go to the toilet, which was luxury compared to the first leg of the journey. We landed at Brize Norton but had to wait on the aircraft, while different regiments and squadrons disembarked and were taken to different areas. There were people everywhere, families of everyone who came back, the Union Jack was being flown or carried by well-wishers.

We were ushered down the aircraft steps onto the pan and across the tarmac, the doors were then opened at one of the terminals and in we went to a very loud rapturous applause, whilst we were met by our families. The first person I saw was Mel, she had a big smile on her face, she was looking very radiant wearing a white top, and rings on her fingers; she came up gave me a hug and a kiss, mum then came over to hug me too. Dad, as cool as ever waited for the ladies to finish, before coming over and shaking my hand, he then said how much everyone was looking forward to me returning. I asked dad how they got to Brize, as none of them could drive?

He told me that the squadron kept in constant touch with them and arranged a lift by MT to Odiham, they then flew over to Brize by Chinook. After a brief handshake and chat with OC Supply who flew over with them. We were told to board the Chinook waiting on the pan for our final flight home.

We landed back at Odiham and went straight to the armoury to hand in our weapons; in the meantime, my dad gathered up my kit and placed it into the back of the Sherpa van. SAC Tony Benn was our driver, he volunteered to work late to drive us home to Croydon, he was a Supplier, the same as me.

As we drove, we just chatted for the 1-hour journey up the M3, we arrived at about 7.00 pm. Outside my mum and dads house were banners with "welcome home" on and a Union Jack was hanging out of the upstairs window. Mitch was at the door to greet me, she had arrived earlier in the day but unfortunately, the RAF would not let her travel over, due to limited numbers.

Mum and dads house was a Victorian end of terrace house on a south London side street, and very typical of all the dwellings in this area. There was a row of shops just yards away and a couple of pubs over the road.
Mum and dad bought the house in 1968 and paid £1000 for it; and it went for a song when we sold it!

I now had 6 weeks off on stand down. With 3 months' pay in my bank, it wasn't long before that started to dwindle, I bought a car, as mine was written off when I was away! I paid £275 for a maroon D Registration MK 1 Ford Cortina, which was about 17 years old. Mel and I spent the next few weeks driving around in it visiting everyone.

The railway tavern was a pub in Carshalton where we all drank, Mel's dad and sister could be found behind the bar sometimes. Like Mel's parents, the landlord and his wife were both ex RAF, and their daughter, Sharon was currently serving and joined up about the same time as me. They had raised a few hundred pounds for the South Atlantic fund by doing some charity events. So, laid on a press presentation with the local rag; Sharon presented me with a cheque, the press had a field day when it was published, it made out that I "yomped" with 2 Para across the island to take Stanley, what a load of bollocks. I told them the truth and they just wrote what they wanted to write.

During the evening I was introduced to a lot of people; this was my local, but who were they, I didn't know, probably hangers-on, or new to the area and adopted the

Tavern as their new watering hole, after all, I had been away for a long time.

Some of the lads that were friends with my soon-to-be brother in law, who I also knew, wanted to stash 4 tyres in the boot of my Cortina, as it was the only car there at the time. Just as we shut the boot a cop car pulled up and asked to see what we were doing, I was shitting myself, because while serving in the military if you get done by the civvy cops you stood a good chance of being done by the Feds back at base. I opened my boot, as the copper looked in he saw all my military kit, webbing, boots and helmet; he immediately asked what that was, my future brother in law pipped up and said: "We were celebrating his return from the Falklands and I just bought the tyres off him". He said, "carry on and have a good night". F*cking lucky to get away with that.

Back inside, one couple in their thirties or forties started talking to me and said why they were there that night, I think they were related to someone in the pub; they mentioned that they had family in the Falklands who were also at Port San Carlos, it turned out it was John and Mandy!

The Falklands War for me was personal, not that it had anything to do with the hatred of the enemy, no I didn't, they were just following orders as we were; it was political bullying, someone high up trying to take something that was not theirs. This small settlement

117

8000 miles from the UK, that I had not even heard of 5 months ago, would be part of me for the rest of my life. Two hundred and fifty-five British military personnel, 649 Argentine military personnel and 3 Falkland Islanders died during the hostilities.

One hundred and thirty-two aircraft were lost, and 6 British and 8 Argentine ships were sunk.

The British ships were:

HMS Sheffield.
HMS Ardent
HMS Antelope
HMS Coventry
SS Atlantic Conveyor
RFA Sir Galahad

CHAPTER 7

Marriage and posting

One year after the Falklands war, Mel and I got married and move into Airman's Married Quarters (AMQ) in Church Crookham, Fleet. We had to pick the hottest day of the year for the wedding. I was cursed by my best man and the other RAF lads, as I made us all wear full No.1 dress uniform for the occasion.

At one point during the reception, the lads picked me up and tried to throw me fully clothed and still in uniform into a swimming pool, luckily for me the door was locked.

Even though we were partying, we still had to have our wits about us, or at least one of us did and wasn't me or Pete, my bestie. The last thing we wanted was unwanted attention as we were all in uniform and the club we used was used by some known people from a Northern Irish descent.

There were over 200 people in the hall, we probably knew only about 50 or 60, some were Sean's friends' others were my dad's.

Two of my dad's blagged an invite by saying they would video record the day's proceedings; I only hope my dad didn't pay for it! Pair of cowboys with a new toy.

The next day we loaded up my Vauxhall Viva and went to start it; nothing, no ignition, no power. Then after a few minutes of playing about with it, I managed to get it started, and we headed off to Carshalton from our hotel in Sutton where we spent our wedding night. We arrived outside the Railway tavern and saw the priest that married us come out of the church opposite, we went over to thank him, but when we got back in the car, it failed to start again. Father Zammit, stood in front of my bonnet, did the Sign of The Cross and blessed the car. I turned the key and it started the first time.

We have no idea how he did that, but it got us home to Fleet.

The AMQ estate was built in the late sixties by Barrett or Wimpey Homes and were situated in the village. There was a local pub just a few minutes' walk, and behind the estate was a NAAFI shop, which was shared with Queen Elizabeth barracks which was the home of Gurkha Rifles. The Gurkhas were real gentleman but also real warriors, who also served in the Falklands. Every morning at about 7.00 Mel would leave for work and on her way to the bus stop; the Gurkhas would be on their morning tab, as each rank of 3 passed the bus stop, they would turn their heads in Mel's direction and say "good morning ma'am" and carry on with their tab down the hill.

Mel was a qualified electronic solderer and assembler, there a few factories around that wanted her services, so was lucky to find employment quickly.

Just over 2 years later, I got my first overseas posting to West Germany.

It was February 85, the snow had covered the area, and I was preparing and loading the car, ready for the long solo drive to Germany. I was due to catch a ferry in a couple of days, so I was spending a bit of time at home. Mel had popped out and I was sitting around as I had already cleared from Odiham when there was a knock on the door; I opened it and got covered in snowballs, some of our friends from around the estate were having a snowball fight, I had no choice but to retaliate. After about half-hour of larking about, we all returned to our quarters.

They were a great bunch of guys and girls, everyone got on well and partied well too.

A little after Mel got home, I realised I couldn't find my car keys anywhere and I had no spare. I had to break a window in the car to get the door open and had to go and buy a new ignition switch, which I managed to replace myself, it cost about £30, but we didn't have a lot of money. Mel was well pissed off with me. The next morning a lady came to the door and asked if I owned a Lancia, as she had found a set of keys in the melting snow, the key had a Lancia logo, I got lucky. I managed to get some of the money back but had to endure a winters' drive across Europe with a broken window and only a piece of cardboard held onto the car with bodge tape

I was back in a barrack block in a foreign country, I didn't know a soul, these were massive dormitory's with all different trades sleeping all on different shifts, all waiting for more permanent single accommodation or married quarters. The block was just behind the bank near the Malcolm Club. I started work the next day and reported to the main Supply Admin on 431 Maintenance Unit which was situated on thew main base, RAF Bruggen.

RAF Bruggen was in the village of Elmpt about 27 miles from Dusseldorf, part of the station was in no man's land on the Dutch border.

Bruggen was the main base flying Tornadoes from four squadrons based there, it was the main tornado force in NATO.

My new role was to be working with armourers at 3 Base Ammunition Depot or 3 BAD for short. The suppliers consisted of 1 Sgt, 2 Cpls and about 5 SAC's plus a few armourers.

The base had a 26km perimeter making it the largest ammo depot in Europe.

The site which is now a nature reserve had lots of wildlife including deer and wild boar. The wild boar used to chase us when we were driving our Rough Terrain Forklift Trucks (RTFL). We could spend all day out on the RTFL's moving bombs around, it was great in the summer, but not so good in the winter.

I finally managed to get an AMQ, which would be a private hiring. Locals used to rent out properties to the British Forces, your parent unit would allocate as they saw fit. And the properties were usually a lot better than the standard accommodation you could get.

I came back to Church Crookham to help Mel pack up the house ready for the move. The removals van had left already, just in time for our last house party!

The homebrew was flowing and was in every corner of the house. Half the squadron singlies were there and most of our married friends from around the patch. The idea of the party was to get everyone to help clean up the mess ready for us to" march-out". In the military when you hand something back it must be in the same or better condition than when you got it. In the case of an AMQ, even small things like leaving a picture hook in the wall would land you a fine, the fine they say is to pay someone to put it right. I bet the families officers and barrack wardens have a great Christmas 'piss-up' in the mess every year. Mel pulled it off, what a great idea, the" march-out" went without too many snags and no fine.

We loaded the Lancia, and got ready for the long drive, I had replaced the window with a piece of perspex, which I cut one day during some downtime on the bomb dump, and was worried that it would hold and keep out the winter breeze; it worked a treat

We arrived in Bruggen village in the evening and stayed over in a B&B; the Families Officer was due to March us into the AMQ about 0900. We arrived early at about 0800. We were sitting in the car waiting, listening to BFBS on the radio when there was a sudden bang on the roof of the car. A tall chap stood there looking in "Hello my name is Alex" he said," do you want some breakfast, Bev's done a fry up". Well, that was it, we had just made the best friends you could ever want to meet. Alex was a Sgt techie also working at 431MU, at RAF Bruggen, though this was the first time that we had met. He was a tall broad-shouldered guy, someone who when you first meet you think to yourself; I don't want to mess with this guy. It turned out that he wasn't far off being a black belt in Taekwondo (TKD), he also studied other martial arts. TKD is a Korean martial art, which is practised by their armed forces; he would soon introduce me to TDK too. Beverley is a character and so suited to Alex, also tall, she holds a black belt in cooking and making cocktails. They had the flat upstairs and we resided down. We were only Brits on the street and we were surrounded by the Germans, who I must say, we all got along very well with.

We had the next six months with our new friends before they were posted back to the UK. We keep in contact with each other and get together for weekends when we can where the booze, food and banter continue.

In January 86' the landlord decided that he was going to take back the building from the RAF and let it out to civilians instead. Rather than stay until the end of the contract, we decided to move into the AMQ flats in Elmpt. But this meant Mel having to give up her job in the Outback club (NAAFI) on the army base, where she served the squaddies beer and sandwiches at the bar.

The new flat was OK and overlooking a communal car park with other blocks surrounding it. All the flats had an illegal cellar bar which the RAF Feds frequently tried to close down.

Mel soon got a job in the Sgts Mess at RAF Bruggen, and I continued on the bomb dump for about 18 months before getting transferred to 431 MU Supply.

This was better for me as I was still playing football but was also now a blue belt in TKD. I then got told that the TKD instructor was being posted; I tried to hold the club together for a couple of months with simply basic stuff but no sparring. In the end, I had to let it go and embark on a new adventure.

My C.O. wanted me to try out for a mountain expedition; it would go in my favour when the promotion board sat. This expedition would help show leadership and initiative. There were 14 of us trying out, but only 7 would go. After a few weeks of training in the evenings, we were given the go-ahead for a move to Bavaria, to do some serious mountain work, before selection for the final climb – The Zugspitze!

During a 10 day stay in the Bavarian Alps, I wondered what it would be like to do mountain warfare and be part of an SF unit; one of the guys with us had been through selection training with the SAS but had failed twice and had been kicked off. He was super fit and looked the part, that put me off thinking about that any further, there was absolutely no way I would complete selection, and being RAF, I would get so much shit thrown at me, I'm not sure if any RAF had ever applied or even passed.

I was one of the 7 chosen to do the climb; it was the middle of March, the weather was perfect, and we were told that in 2 days, we were off. We spent the next day on leisure and practising our abseiling techniques.

It was only when we were on our way that we were told about some of the hazards on the climb, something that we should have known about before. The first was," the spikes", these were about 300 m up the 2962m mountain. There were about 20 steel spikes that had been hammered into the rock face about 2 feet apart, a cable also followed this trajectory at waist height, to enable the climber to attach a carabiner. The spikes went from right to left on a slight incline on a curve. In other words, we couldn't see the end.

Our base camp was in a town called Garmisch Partenkirchen, which is very popular with skiers.

We arrived at the foot of the mountain at about 0600hrs, did a radio check and adjusted our kit. It was a warm morning and the sun was shining. We were at the foot of a valley which had rocks everywhere, which were being used as steppingstones through the valley which was once filled with water from a waterfall. You could see most of the mountain, except for the summit which had a cloud over it. We were led by one of the teams who took us to the first staging point, which was given to us by our leader; then someone else would take the over, it was planned that all the staging posts would be approximately one hour apart. On my lead, like a good football coach, I decided that we would go in a 2, 3, 2 formation. I was to lead off with my number 2. Whoever lead would run a commentary all the way letting the team know what was happening and any hazards that you may come across, the groups were quite spread out and travelling at their own speed but also concentrating on their own surroundings. I imagine that this is what mountain warfare would be like, except we were not carrying weapons.

The first hazard had quickly approached me, the dreaded spikes. Not one bit, I just carried on, one spike at a time, then I came upon a gap; a spike was missing. I called back to warn the team. We all passed with no issues then I came to a sudden stop. Then a second set of spikes, except instead of them going at the same rate of ascent as the first, these were at a different rate which involved us stepping across and up at the same time. This was hard work; I was now using muscles that I didn't know I had. Eventually, we came to a safe area where we could rest, with the spikes now behind us, I didn't fancy doing that again.

On someone else's lead, we stopped for a brief at the start of a glacier. The boss was going to lead on this and gave strict instructions to follow in a straight line at 2 metres apart (social distancing if you like).

"Follow my footprints in the snow, don't deviate, where I step, you step". He repeated the statement, to make sure we all understood.

"Any question?" we all stood in silence.

"Ready to move. Move" was the next instruction, we slung on our backpacks and followed.

It was very sunny and bright; the snow was covering about 100 metres on an uphill slant. There were other groups up ahead of us, and another just getting off the glacier. Suddenly there was a shout from the rear of our group" STOP, MAN DOWN". F*ck, I thought. What's happening. We stood still. The message came up the line that one of our team had stepped out of line, literally and had fallen down a hole in the snow. The hole was about 3ft wide at the opening, and went down about 20ft, narrowing all the way down. We traced our footsteps back, regrouped and managed to pull him out. Luckily, he was wearing his backpack as that wedged him in, it had to one of the armourers, no stacker would pull that off. After a stern bollocking from the boss for deviating off the course, we continued to the end of the glacier.

The next obstacle to endure was the ladder. There was a 4-metre vertical climb up the next face. The ladder runs were a series of metal steps that were put in place to get to the final stretch up to the summit. Where the glacier floor ended there was a drop of about 100 foot into some rocks, to get on the ladder you had to step over the gap and onto the first rung, then climb. The first couple of guys got up, then it was my turn. I just froze, maybe I shouldn't have looked down, and it didn't help that there was a plaque on the rock face, 'Here fell' with the name of a British Army Captain and the date of his demise. I broke the first major rule for rock climbers, I looked down, I started to hyperventilate and shake. I couldn't reach up to get on the first run. The same guy who f*cked up earlier when he fell in the glacier hole came to the rescue. He removed my kit and throw it on his back, whilst he and another helped me get over this obstacle and up onto the first rung. Ever since this incident, I have been scared of heights. We finished the climb in just under 8 hours.

At the summit was a viewing area with the cable car to go back down. There was a small cafeteria which sold sandwiches and postcards printed with the views over Austria and prints of the spikes, ladder and the glacier. They even sold beer. We threw our kit in a pile in a corner and sat down to admire the views. The boss went and bought 7 steins of Heineken, which had gone down so quickly that they came back up just as fast.

We packed up and headed to the base camp before our journey back through Bavaria and into West Germany and then back to Bruggen for a weekend off.

I returned to work on the Monday, but not long after we had been back at camp, the security alert had changed due to a political incident with America and Libya. A bomb had exploded in a Berlin discotheque killing 2 and injuring dozens more, mostly American servicemen who used the facilities regularly. Libya practically admitted it; this was followed by airstrikes ordered by Ronald Reagan on Tripoli and Benghazi. So not only were we now protecting the base against the Russians and IRA, we also had the Middle East to look out for.

Our security was on point, it was drummed into us about awareness and surroundings. If we went out in a group one man would be sober and "lookout" usually also the duty driver. We never went to the same place at the same time, we altered our routes, and watched our 6s'. (Keeping a watch behind). Even today, if we go to a restaurant or pub, I will sit where I can see the door, I watch who comes and who goes. Through this observation, I have witnessed many behaviours of some certain dodgy people, which I won't go into.

The IRA started to step up their game, we had intel, that they were operating cells in Europe, the main trouble was, knowing where they were, it didn't help, that we (RAF Bruggen) and 2 other RAF bases were on the Dutch border and it was easy to cross.

Just after we were posted back, news came through that the IRA had killed 3 RAF Regiment guys outside a café in Roermond, just over the border from RAF Bruggen.

They also shot an off-duty airman whilst he was filling up his car, his daughter was also murdered as she sat in the car. And an army wife was shot at point-blank range in her car outside her married quarter, she was hit with 12 rounds.

CHAPTER 8

1990's and second Falkland's tour

Back in the UK and with me now a Corporal we settled into our new AMQ at RAF Brampton. In 1990, Mel had just given birth to our son when the Gulf War One kicked off. There were a lot of complications with Patrick and he spent the next few months in and out of Hospital. Mel didn't drive and public transport in our area was non-existent. Luckily, I had a great Sergeant, Gordon Bailey, who let me have as much time as needed. Gordon was a great guy, who loved his sport, he was into football and tennis. He also used to be a Service Steward at the All England Lawn Tennis Association at Wimbledon, which he introduced me to. Getting involved with this used up two weeks annual leave every summer but I got paid for it. I was lucky as mum and dads house was only 3 miles away, so I could spend a few nights with them especially if I had an early shift. I went on to do this every year until I left the RAF, working in the Royal Box meeting and greeting, 'A' list celebrities, tennis players, politicians and members of the Royal Family.

My duties at the tournament were to look after the members area in the Royal Box on centre court. It was here that I got to meet and mingle with many sports stars and celebrities. My area within the Royal Box was the members area which housed the female top 10 seeded players' changing area and reception. The members that used this exclusive area where past winners or had some other affiliation with the club like Sir Cliff Richard and Charlton Heston. I had a team of 8 in my team with a mix from all 3 services. This was also the area where the Close Protection (CP) team hung out. My area was above the men's top 10 changing area, where the likes of Andre Agassi and Tim Henman all hung out; the ladies area had Venus and Serena Williams, Lindsey Davenport, and my favourite Steffi Graff.

The area is in a very exclusive part of the Royal Box; to get to it there was a private entrance to the left of the Royal Box's main entrance on the ground floor. I cannot possibly write about some of the things that I witnessed due to the libellous actions that would be taken against me. However, without name dropping, a particular top-10 seeded female European player was dating another European sports star of another sport; the tabloid newspapers had been hounding them for a few days and were looking for a story. It was quarter final day in the men's championship and some of the ladies were not playing.

It was my turn on the main door. I opened it to let Sir Cliff in and he told me that the press had got in downstairs, I then spotted the female player and her boyfriend having a snog on the stairs; the press would have had a field day with a picture of them embracing each other; they were closing in fast! I managed to grab her by the arm and pull her into the secure area with her boyfriend so she would not be snapped. The CP team then removed the press for me.

She thanked me for what I did and later that day she brought in some strawberries and cream for the team.

But in January 91 I was called in to see my boss, he gave me the news that we knew was coming, I was to be put on standby for deployment to the Gulf. I spent the next week getting kit ready, I had a medical, NBC refresher course and, at one point, I had to go to RAOC Bicester to collect more appropriate clothing. On arrival I was greeted by a L/Cpl from the RLC (Royal Logistics Corp) who I knew from my time at Bracht, he took me to where I had to go. I knocked on the Clothing Store's' door and was met by one of my old FSs', Mick Harber from Odiham; he was expecting me. We chewed the cud for a while and we spoke fondly of our time there. We said our goodbyes and I climbed back into the MT vehicle that I had signed out and returned to Brampton. When I got home, Mel presented me with a letter from the hospital, Patrick was to be admitted in a couple of weeks to have surgery.

This wasn't a good time for us, we had no family nearby to help, we just had to get on with it. My only choice was to see if I could be taken off standby this would mean someone else would have to go in my place.

I put in my Gen App and passed it to my boss. The Gen App or General Application which is a form of communication to the higher authorities if you wish to apply for something in particular; most of the time they would be granted. Luckily for me, it was.

Patrick's operation was a success. The rest of the year went by without any incidents or dramas. In 1992, my name came to the top of the list for overseas detachment again, this time there were hospital appointments or other deployments. I was told that I was going back to the Falklands, but this time with a difference.

I flew out on a VC10 and landed back on the Islands that I had helped liberated 10 years before. Other than the new airfield at RAF Mount Pleasant, in Stanley everything looked the same as it was 10 years before, stuck in a time warp!

My job in Forward Supply was to coordinate the distribution of stores as they arrived by air, around the base for all 3 services and also to a few remote areas around the islands, if we couldn't drive to them, we would arrange for heli-lifts. We were a 7-man team which consisted of a Sgt (RAF), myself as 2 I/C, a L/Cpl from the RLC and a private, 2 SACs and an LSA from the Navy. We had at our disposal 2 land rovers, a JCB forklift truck, which was the same as I learned to use at Bracht and a couple of 4 tonners.

One entitlement on deployment, was LOA (local overseas allowance), this is a payment in lieu of salary to help you get by and R and R (Rest and Recuperation), the more tours you got to the Falklands, resulted in more days R and R, at least that was what was supposed to happen. Troops on their first tour were entitled to 3 or 4 days at the halfway point, as this was my second, I was given 10 days.

My R and R was arranged by PSF, I had no say, but was so glad it happened. My halfway point was the anniversary of the surrender by Argentina. It was arranged for me and 9 others (all Falklands veterans) to attend the 10th-anniversary events on the Islands. We boarded HMS Bampton Castle and spent a few days sailing around the islands, we visited all the war graves of the ships that were sunk and also to Blue Beach

Military Cemetery, this was where 2 Para had landed. We then attended a remembrance parade, before being stood down, I spent the rest of my R and R visiting John and Mandy who were now living in Stanley. I returned home in August.

Tensions were high again with the IRA, more bombing on the UK mainland and also some killings abroad. We were having to be more cautious about what we did and how did it. We were checking under our cars before every journey, looking out for suspicious packages and bags, and never doing the same route twice in succession.

One sunny weekend morning I was guard commander, a nice easy duty to contend with; just handing out keys and making sure the patrols went out on time and ensuring that they followed their weapon drills on return from patrol. The Ord Sgt had gone somewhere to deal with a compassionate case as someone's mum had died, he had to go and break the news and arrange transport for the poor lad. The orderly officer had come to the guardroom to inspect some defaulters who were given 'Jankers', a military term for punishment, usually for a minor offence. The Officer was a young sprog about 6-foot-tall and ginger hair and still wet behind the ears, this was his first posting after graduating out of Cranwell.

We were chatting and passing the time, when the radio clicked on, it had been quiet for a while with not even a radio check. It turns out that they had stumbled across something and wanted to check it before reporting back. The conversation would have gone something like:

"Charlie one this is Alpha one, message over".
"Alpha one go ahead".
The patrol leader went on to say,
"suspicious package sighted at grid reference blah blah blah, at officers married quarters electricity substation over"
"Alpha One, this is Charlie one, wait out"

I turned to the OO (Orderly Officer) to brief him. He didn't have a clue, he wasn't sure what to do next, there was an Aide Memoire hanging in the guardroom which is supposed to be read when you went on duty, he clearly didn't. I took charge of the incident, he just had to trust my instincts and training.

I decided to grab my weapon and radio, and take the OO with me, he was unarmed, thank f*ck. We proceeded over to the area to check it out.

By some of the houses was the substation, it was about 4 m sq, with a small picket fence around it and a normal garden gate to the entrance which had a small step down, the gate was not padlocked. Low underneath this generator looking thing in the middle was a black briefcase, handle facing outwards and a single closed latch in the middle.

I immediately radioed back to the guardroom to get a message to the Station Commander his contact details would be held by COMCEN and MT would immediately despatch a driver to pick him up. It turned out that he was away with his family for the weekend. So, another senior rank was informed.

I returned to the guardroom and immediately contacted the emergency services, who in turn called the EOD team up at RAF Wittering just up at M1.

The local roads were closed off and the A1 heading south between Brampton Hut and Kimbolton had a lane closed off to allow the emergency services to move freely. My proudest moment to date was getting all the local roads closed off!

It took a few hours to get things in place, I had handed over to the EOD commander who took charge. I was at the EOD van which is now the ops room, watching on a small black and white tv screen, there was no sound just a crackled distorted picture which was being relayed back from the robot to the van.

The robot was a small wheelbarrow type of machine which instead of wheels, had two tank tracks and the turret which held a shotgun that's used to fire off a special cartridge which holds water, and a camera; this is operated by remote control from the ops van.

On first inspection as the robot manoeuvred into position, it fell over the step and toppled onto its side. The controller not panicking and keeping calm, managed to use its shotgun arm to right itself back into position. He lined the machine up ready to fire. "standby, standby" he announced over the radio. "ready to fire, FIRE" as that last word was spoken, he pressed on a button and BANG! The cartridge went off, a small puff of smoke and water all over the briefcase. An EOD guy, dressed in all his leaf armour protecting his bits, approached the area. The radio clicked and the message "Stand-down Stand-down", he came back to the van with the briefcase, it's contents soaked in water, there were copies of Shoot magazine and some soft porn magazines, it must have belonged to one of the officers children , we never did find out.

CHAPTER 9

RAF Northolt and NATO HQ.

Now living in West Ruislip on the AMQ patch, Mel fell pregnant and later gave birth to our daughter. Northolt had just suffered a tragedy when one of our pay clerks was found dead on her doorstep after a night out with all of us in the Sports and Social. She never turned up for work, her Sgt went to the flats opposite the camp gate. She lived on the top floor, where she was found, key still in her hand.

The station went into mourning, and I was chosen to be a pallbearer for her. The funeral was very stressful. We had to carry the coffin into the Station Chapel, her coffin was draped in the Union flag, with WRAF Hat and medals placed neatly on top. The problem we had was getting through the Chapel door as it was only just over 6 ft high. We had the coffin on our shoulders and had to duck down to make sure we cleared the top without losing her military regalia. The day went well, and we returned to normal duties the following day.

Italy was my next detachment, but there was drama at home on the evening I was to fly out. I had packed all my kit and was having a final soak in the bath when my daughter decided to slice the top of her finger on a tin of sweetcorn. She ran up the stairs to me screaming, quickly followed by Mel and Patrick shouting at her not touch the walls – too late blood everywhere! It looked like a scene out of a Hitchcock thriller. She entered the bathroom and my nice bath turned claret. So, we spent the next few hours in A and E, I had to pull my ace to try and jump the queue as my transport would soon be picking me up.

In true RAF fashion, my new home was a 4-star hotel in Conversarno, in the Hotel D'Arragona a few miles outside Bari near the Adriatic Sea. Six months in the sun, supporting air ops with the Harriers, flying over the Former Yugoslavia.

The Harriers were operating out of Italy's premier Air Force base, Gioia Del Col, which we had to commute to daily; about a 30 minute drive through some of Italy's most sandy roads, driving past golden sandy olive groves and picturesque vineyards.

Stationed here, I became a lover of red wine; I was always a beer drinker, but after visiting some of the vineyards and wine tasting, I got hooked. Some of the best reds come from the Puglia region, which was about an hour's drive to the "heel" of the country.

I spent most of my time in the sun, I was on a week about shift, nights then day, but the rain was so bad over the Adriatic Sea, most sorties were abandoned and we were stood down. That gave me a chance to spend some time snorkelling or playing football.

I managed to get Mel out for a week during my R and R, other than that trip on a Chinook when I returned from the Falklands, it was the first time she had ever flown on a plane and she was on her own. We had a great week in the karaoke and pizza bars and managed to visit Rome and Naples.

The following year (1997), I lost my dad, he had been in hospital for a couple of weeks and on the morning of Good Friday, when he was about to be discharged; his heart stopped and he was gone. Ironically, he had got up, had a shower and was standing by his bed having some banter with some patients and that was it. He was just 66.

The last time I saw him alive was 2 weeks before on St Patrick's day, his 66 birthday; he came to look after Tamara as Patrick had a hospital appointment. That evening, dad came with me to get some fish and chips, whilst I was paying he disappeared into the shop next door and bought a bottle of brandy, he said: "we'll do this tonight son". That was our last drink together and our last conversation. He died a few days later after a short illness in hospital.

Five months later the world was shocked at the loss of Diana, the Princess of Wales. We were fast asleep when Patrick woke us up and said "the Princess is dead" I am very patriotic and this hit me, it brought back thoughts of my dad.

The next day, we were on the side of the runway at RAF Northolt as Princess Diana's coffin was taken off the aircraft by members of the Queens Colour Squadron before she was repatriated with the Royal Family, a memory that will stay with us for life.

The following year I was posted to NATO HQ, just up the road at Northwood, so we did not have to move. I was part of a two-man procurement team, me and a Flt Lieutenant (Flt Lt) plus several NATO civilians from all different NATO countries. I collected my new ID card which stated my name rank and number, but instead of saying Royal Air Force, it said United Kingdom Air Force (UKAF) this also applied to Army (UKA) and Navy (UKN) personal. All staff would wear a shield which represented CINC Eastlant Commander In Chief East Atlantic, which was part of SACLANT (Supreme Allied Commander Atlantic), which was based in Norfolk Virginia, USA. Even though I was now under these big headliners, I was still paid by the MOD and all my personnel administration was now conducted at RAF Uxbridge.

In 1999, we decided that we should buy our own place, I was due out in 3 years anyway. So, we started house hunting, Ruislip and the surrounding towns was way out of our price range, we started looking further afield. Eventually we found a mock Tudor house, in Leagrave, just outside Luton. Three months later, we moved in.

My days with NATO were spent, buying equipment, and setting up contracts working 9-5, it was a different kind of job, but also quite mundane.

On one particular day, what had started as a normal day had changed significantly when I had got back from my lunch. My boss came in and told me that the Yanks were all in a flap in the officer's mess as an aircraft had just flown into the World Trade Centre. Not really knowing much about this building and what it represented, I went about my business. I took a walk down the corridor and immediately noticed it's stillness, quite eerie really, and as I passed the Intelligence Office, I noticed it was packed to the rafters with different uniforms and civvies alike. I saw one of my oppos who ushered me in. I looked at the monitors on the back wall that everyone was looking at and a moment later we witnessed the second aircraft hit one of the towers. We were getting live streams back from Washington DC, and then watching Sky News coverage seconds later.

These events were to change NATO and the world forevermore. Our security was once again at risk.

The HQ, the Atlantic building, was a 4-storey building that was built for NATO Staff right in the centre of the base. Three floors were visible, and one was underground, this underground part of the building led through underground corridors into JSSU ops room, which is manned 24/7. This is the same JSSU room that Mrs Thatcher controlled the Falklands war from.

The main gate to the base was manned by armed Royal Marines (RM). To get into Atlantic building you had to pass through two security barriers, which were manned by one UKAF Cpl (Tom) and 2 MOD Police, all unarmed.

NATO is its own entity; we were not allowed to use MOD equipment or money to run it. The C in C decided that we needed to protect the building and staff, plans had already been drawn up in case of an attack against us. The plans included the guards to be armed, and because of the NATO ruling, we were not allowed to use MOD property including the weapons held at RAF Uxbridge to protect the building. After the daily Orders Group, it was decided that only the building guards would be armed, as the perimeter was already controlled by the RM's.

As procurement I was called in to see one of the senior UKN Commanders, he asked: "have you ever procured arms before"? "No", I said, I only used to move them. "Well Corporal, no time like the present to start". He passed me a list of equipment. Two of everything; Kevlar vests; holsters; spare magazines; cleaning kits and 2 Browning 9mm pistols. It had been arranged that the RMs would provide the ammunition.

I managed to get the vests and holsters quite easy from a supplier used by the MOD. I had to near beg my opposite number at the UK MOD procurement office in Bristol to help.

For the weapons, we had to jump through all sorts of hoops, eventually, I got an order through to an office in Belgium.

This all had to be verified and approved at a high level first. Once this was all complete, I was given an airway bill number and instructions on how to collect it once it arrived in the UK.

The following morning Tom and I met at RAF Uxbridge, he signed out a sidearm and I signed out a vehicle, the MT request forms stated, the purpose of journey "restricted NATO Duties", well that was a first, I was not expecting that, normally Uxbridge are not that accommodating; we found out later that the Air Commodore had called in a favour. We set off across West London heading for a lockup customs office hidden on an industrial estate, somewhere in Hounslow. We arrived soon after showed our NATO IDs and Airway Bill, we were ushered to a cage and I was swiped in, Tom waited outside.

I showed my ID again and a MOD guard took my airway bill to an office in the back. Not long after a guy in army combats with no rank badges showing, brought a box to me and asked me to break the seal. On opening it, I pulled out 2 bags buried deep in packaging material. In each bag was one browning pistol wrapped in hessian. I opened each package in turn, checked the work parts and serial numbers then sealed them back in their boxes and left the cage. Tom and I secured the packages under the passenger seat of the Land Rover and headed back to base via a McDonald's drive-through. We arrived back at Northwood, handed in the weapons and returned the Land Rover to RAF Uxbridge. That was us for the day, so we both went home to talk about our adventure.

I arrived back at work the next day on my NTV600 motorcycle, it was a beautiful day and a great ride down the M1 from Luton. Just as I was about to get out of my leathers, I was summoned in to see the Air Commodore, thinking to myself he wanted to thank me for yesterday; I went and waited outside his office, still in my leathers and carrying my crash helmet. Tom was already waiting there.

The door opened and in we went, we stood to attention in front of his desk. He had a large office also on the top floor, but he was in an area where all the officers had their offices. The window overlooked the car park.

He was stood looking out of the window with his hands behind his back. "At ease you two and take a seat". He turned and sat at his big desk. "Thank you both for doing that job yesterday, the CINC can sleep better at night, knowing he has 2 MOD plods protecting his building," he said with a smirk on his face. I had a feeling that he wasn't too confident with this kind of protection. He then looked at me and said: "what did you not do yesterday, Corporal." I was dumbstruck, I didn't have a clue what he was talking about. "Sorry Sir, I'm not sure" I replied.

He stood up leant forward on his desk and barked "You forget to inform the f*cking Met (Metropolitan Police) that you were driving around London whilst carrying weapons." My heart sunk, I felt sick in the mouth. I had moved weapons around the UK and abroad many times before and I had never f*cked up. He sat back down and smiled and said. "it was a good job that someone had your backs". It was standard operating procedures by the RLC guys back in the cage in Hounslow, they had informed the Met, but ultimately it was my responsibility to pass on my route and ETA which I didn't do.

Not long after 9/11, I was selected on the promotion board for promotion to the rank of Sgt which I duly accepted. My goal in the RAF was to reach the rank of Cpl and do at least 12 years. I was now a Sgt and closing in on completing 22 years; I had fulfilled my ambition.

I completed my promotion courses at RAF Halton and was lucky enough to remain in my current post at NATO, where I was working on a NATO project to implement a new travel system/procurement system, I had a lot of time to think about my future. Just before my discharge date, I was offered the chance to sign on until I was 47. NATO had also offered me a 12-month contract should I leave the RAF. I had made my decision; I was leaving the RAF, I did my full term.

I got my Three Stripes, I'm out"

The End!

Epilogue

These were vivid memories of all those years in the RAF which I have shared. Yet I find it hard to remember things that happened more recently.

I realise now that school set me up for that journey, even though I did not enjoy my education.

My time in the military showed me what the world was all about, I visited some amazing places, and met some amazing people from different walks of life and cultures. It taught me discipline, respect, and dignity.

Nowadays I can sit and in my garden with my family and friends and reminisce.

We sat here in the sunshine enjoying a pint listening to some of our favourite songs.

I am on stage at the end of the garden, guarding the BBQ, when I hear the distant sound of beating rotor blades and that sound of a Chinook helicopter in the distance. With a lump in my throat, I look up and raise a glass, but there is nothing there; yet the sound is getting louder. I don't understand it's a warm summer evening the sky is blue and not a cloud to be seen. I looked back at my family feeling a bit confused, but they are sitting at the garden bar watching me, Patrick can't stop himself from laughing, they are all rolling about on the AstroTurf as the rotor blade sound starts to fade, then the strum of a guitar chord is heard as the tune from the group Oasis blasting out the song "What's the story, morning glory".

The sound of those rotor blades bashing in the wind will stay with me forevermore.

Would I do it all again? Yes.

Glossary

4 TONNER — Bedford 4 tonne lorry

BATTALION — Military formation of around 600 strong in the army

CHARGE — Form F252 – The start of a disciplinary procedure in the military

CHINOOK — Large twin rotor helicopter is capable of carrying up 10 tonnes

D.I. — Drill Instructor

EOD — Explosive and Ordnance Disposal, i.e., bomb disposal

GDT — Ground Defence Training

GPMG — General Purpose Machine Gun

HARRIER — Vertical take-off and landing, strike aircraft

JR MESS	Junior Ranks Mess dining facilities for all junior ranks below Sergeant.
LCU	Landing Craft Utility, can carry 100 men
LOADIE	Crewman/Air Load Master
NAAFI	Navy, Army and Air Forces Institute (Bar)
'O' GROUP	Orders group – gathering of officers
OIC	Officer In Charge
OPPO	Friend, buddy
PIT	Military slang for bed space
PUMA	Anglo French built helicopter
SIDEWINDER AIM9L	US built heat-seeking air-ground

SLR	Self-Loading Rifle — standard British Infantry weapon, 7.62mm Semi Automatic
SROs	Station Routine Orders, daily or weekly notices that also have to be obeyed but can change daily.
SSOs	Station Standing Orders — Policy and Procedures or rules and regulations always to be obeyed.
WESSEX	British troop carrying helicopter

APPENDIX A

MV Norland 12000 tonnes Roll on – Roll off ferry used as a troop carrier which included 2 Para, 18 Sqn RAF.

Atlantic Conveyor 14946 tonnes Cunard Container Ship converted into aircraft ferry for Chinooks, Harriers and various helicopters. – Sunk by an Exocet missile fired by an Argentinian Super Etendard.

HMS Fearless 12,120 tonnes Amphibious Warfare Ship 580 crew. 4 LCUs, 4 Surface to Air Missile launchers and 4 40mm guns.

Chinook ZA718 Bravo November. We managed to move 1500 troops, 95 casualties, 650 POW and over 500 tons of cargo. Awarded DFC

Three Stripes, I'm Out

Printed in Great Britain
by Amazon